He Couldn't Have Done it Without Them.
The Men and Women Who Helped Win
the American Revolution

History Lives In These Pages!

If you think of reading history as a dull exercise in memorizing dates and facts, you are in for a surprise. With *George Washington's Unsung Heroes,* it is an adventure as exciting as any story in any book or on TV.

What makes this volume so special? For author Marc Stockwell-Moniz, these short stories—quick visits into the lives of real people—are not about a bunch of historical figures long dead. In fact, it's his family history and these heroes live in his imagination and his heart. Look through the table of contents; you'll see two heroes who have the name of Stockwell.

Marc's enthusiasm for the time of the Revolutionary War, and his love for the country then—and now—makes these stories all the more fascinating. He instills the events with real-life drama and puts flesh and blood on the people he writes about. Just reading these stories you start to get a feeling for what it must have been like to have been alive at such a very important time in history.

Each of the 33 stories is short—just a few pages. They offer 33 glimpses into the soul of our country. Together, they provide a broader picture of the Revolutionary War, life at that time, and the people who lived back then.

George Washington's Unsung Heroes will change the way you think about history and our nation's beginnings. It will make you proud to be in a country with such a proud heritage that you can claim as your own.

Marc Stockwell-Moniz lives history, specifically the American Revolution. A literal Son of the American Revolution born in Cambridge, Massachusetts, where George Washington first took command of the fledgling army, Marc can trace his lineage back to English and French kings. His family has been in America since 1650, fully 126 years before the creation of the United States. For him, reading about history is not an academic subject; it's his family album. When Marc writes about the Revolutionary War, he does not describe historical figures. He describes real people who are his family and friends. Marc graduated from San Diego State University in 1978 with a degree in Journalism, and now lives in Southern California with his wife, Teresa, and their young daughter, Danielle. When he is not writing, he delights in talking to audiences of children and adults about the Revolutionary War and early American history.

GEORGE WASHINGTON'S UNSUNG HEROES

Guide to Cover Drawing

Flags: Top, left to right; the Bunker Hill Flag, flown at the legendary Battle of Bunker Hill, June 17, 1775, Charlestown, Massachusetts. The Stars and Stripes Flag or also known as The Betsy Ross Flag, adopted on June 14, 1777, by a resolution of the Continental Congress. The Grand Union Flag, flew over the Continental Army's encampments at Cambridge and Somerville, Massachusetts. This was the flag which flew when General George Washington first took command of the American forces on July 3, 1775 in Cambridge, Massachusetts.

Flags: Bottom, The Commander-in-Chief's Personal Flag.

Figures: Center, Commander-in-Chief General George Washington

Top left, Major General Henry Knox

Bottom left, Colonel Francis Marion

Top right, Lt. Colonel Tench Tilghman

Bottom right, Sergeant Daniel Stockwell Jr.

Cover Illustration by Teresa Moniz

GEORGE WASHINGTON'S UNSUNG HEROES

Marc J. Stockwell-Moniz

American
Revolution
Publishing

George Washington's Unsung Heroes
Copyright © 2005 Marc Stockwell-Moniz

Published by American Revolution Publishing
12514 Mustang Drive
Poway, California 92064
www.americanrevolutionpublishing.com
www.gwuh.com

Publisher's Cataloguing-in-Publication

Stockwell-Moniz, Marc J.
George Washington's unsung heroes / Marc J. Stockwell-Moniz.
     p. cm.
     Includes bibliographical references and index.
     SUMMARY: Thirty-three stories of unsung heroes of the American Revolution whose actions and sacrifices helped George Washington in winning the American Revolutionary War.
     Audience: Grades 6-12.
     LCCN 2004096842
     ISBN 0-9760948-7-8
     1. United States--History--Revolution, 1775-1783--Biography--Juvenile literature. 2. Heroes--United States--Biography--Juvenile literature. 3. Washington, George, 1732-1799--Juvenile literature. [1. United States--History--Revolution, 1775-1783--Biography. 2. Heroes--United States--Biography. 3. Washington, George, 1732-1799.]   I. Title.

E206.S76 2005   973.3'092'2
                                 QBI04-700500

Printed and bound in the United States of America
Cover illustration by Teresa Moniz
Book Design by Patricia Bacall

Without the help and guidance of the following people this book would not have been possible. First the love and support of my very talented wife, Teresa, for her art work, technical knowledge, patience and unending support of my efforts. The dedication of Dr. Sandra LaFave, professor of philosophy at West Valley College in Saratoga, California, was invaluable. Dr. Sandra LaFave made many thoughtful editorial suggestions and comments. I found her advice welcome and educational. Dr. Joan Giglione, professor of journalism at California State University at Fullerton for her suggestions and support. Longtime friend, journalist and author, Randy Schultz deserves a large debt of gratitude for inspiring me to write about the history that I love. Special thanks are in order to Ellen Reid who helped make this book a reality with her expertise, support and guidance.

Finally, I would like to extend an eternal, heartfelt-gratitude to the men and women who made The United States of America a reality.

*"The Revolution was affected before the war commenced.
The Revolution was in the minds and hearts of the people."*

John Adams: 1818

Dedications

This book is dedicated to my grandfather George W. Stockwell, my wife Teresa,
my parents Frank and Peggy, my daughter Danielle, and her namesake, her
fifth-great grandfather Sergeant Daniel Stockwell Jr., a Revolutionary War Hero.

GEORGE WASHINGTON'S — UNSUNG HEROES

TABLE OF CONTENTS

INTRODUCTION

A Revolution of the People, By the People

The American Revolution of 1775-1783 was a tumultuous event for the four million British subjects who would soon become "Americans." The war would have been unthinkable to the colonists just a decade earlier. They were proud to be part of the greatest empire in the world. Even after the fighting had begun at Lexington and Concord on April 19, 1775, only about one-third of all colonists were in favor of American independence.

The first opposition to British rule started not long after the French and Indian War of 1756-1763. Britain defeated France for the control of Canada. Britain was nearly bankrupt at the end of that war. As a result, the British Parliament decided to tax her American colonies for the defense of America. The Stamp Act of 1765 imposed the first direct tax by Britain on its American colonies.

This policy of "taxation without representation" was the beginning of the end of good relations between Britain and her thirteen colonies. The colonies felt betrayed, and Britain felt justified in her actions. Had not Britain just saved the colonies from the threat of the French and her Indian allies? Neither side would back down. Tensions between Britain and her American colonies escalated. The growing conflict pitted father against son, brother against brother.

Many families were torn apart.

This growing conflict was, in many ways, America's first civil war. However, many people felt ambiguous about joining sides in the fight between the American patriots and the British Crown. Most colonists simply just wanted to tend to their fields or work their trades. But as the patriot force gained momentum, it soon became a force that would literally change the world forever.

Many early patriots are familiar names such as Benjamin Franklin, John Adams, and the most famous of them all, George Washington. Yet the names of many have been lost in our history. These men and women are the unsung heroes of the American Revolution. Their stories are told in this book. Two of the stories I present are of my own family—my fourth great-grandfather, Sergeant Daniel Stockwell Jr., and his younger brother, Major Moses Stockwell. The Stockwell brothers were but two of the people who led the way for a new American nation.

As a direct descendant of an American Revolutionary War hero, I have always been amazed at the sacrifices and the risks that these men and women made for the cause of liberty and a free nation. Most of these patriots came from humble backgrounds and all walks of life. Each hero contributed greatly in the cause of freedom

INTRODUCTION

in his or her own way.

There are also some little known stories of the famous patriots. How many people know that our fifth president, James Monroe, was a wounded battlefield hero at the Battle of Trenton, New Jersey? And how much is generally known about the day-to-day life of the enlisted men in the Continental Army? Fortunately, Joseph Plumb Martin's diary of events offers incredible insights to the daily life of a Revolutionary War soldier. In "George Washington's Unsung Heroes," I bring to life the achievements of the first generation of "free" Americans. These brave individuals, led into battle by the Commander-in-Chief, deserve to be honored, remembered, and recognized for the gift that they left all of us. That gift is The United States of America.

HENRY KNOX-ARTILLERY CHIEF

Henry Knox was an educated man. Before the American Revolution and his career as a major general, Knox was a Boston book dealer. Knox loved to read his books. From books he learned the art of firing a cannon.

Knox was born in Massachusetts in 1750. He joined the militia at age eighteen. He possessed a fine military mind. Unfortunately, a serious hunting accident forced young Knox to leave the militia. He lost part of two fingers. However, when the American Revolution started in his home colony, Knox was literally at the right place at the right time to become the American artillery chief.

On April 19, 1775, after the Battles of Lexington and Concord, Knox volunteered his services to General Artemus Ward, Commander-in-Chief of the Massachusetts militia. Knox rejoined the militia just prior to the epic Battle of Bunker Hill on June 17, 1775.

General Artemus Ward needed a smart man like Knox. During the Battle of Bunker Hill, Knox was in the reconnoitering service and General Ward frequently issued orders based on Knox's reports and insight. When the new American Commander-in-Chief General George Washington of Virginia arrived in Cambridge a few weeks later, Knox met the man who he would follow into battle for eight long years. General Washington saw great promise in Knox. By November 1775, Knox was appointed a colonel in the Continental Army.

Meanwhile in Boston, the American Army was besieging the British Army. The patriots needed more armament. Several days after his promotion, Knox undertook his famous and courageous mission to Fort Ticonderoga, in northern New York. Knox and his

Henry Knox

Transported fifty nine cannons and mortars from Ft. Ticonderoga to Boston, during the siege of Boston.

1 HENRY KNOX – ARTILLERY CHIEF

men traveled nearly 650 miles to secure the fifty nine cannons and mortars for the patriot army. Before leaving Fort Ticonderoga, Knox had forty two sleds constructed for the cannons and mortars. They were pulled by teams of oxen across the frozen Hudson River and the hilly terrain of Massachusetts. Knox's men often had to blaze trails because there were no roads. Colonel Knox and his brave volunteers of the "noble train of artillery" dragged the fifty nine large, siege guns over three hundred miles through the snow and ice for nearly six weeks. They arrived safely back at the American camp by mid-January. The big guns were placed in strategic locations around the small peninsula town of Boston.

On a cold winter evening on March 4, 1776, some of the big guns were dragged by the Americans to a prominent hill overlooking Boston to the south. Dorchester Heights was a hilly area that both the

American and British commanders wanted to fortify. Again, just like at Bunker Hill, the Americans beat the British to this strategic location. The redoubts on Dorchester Heights were built with the aim of forcing the enemy to attack the American lines. On February 26, 1776, General Washington wrote: "I am preparing to take a post on Dorchester Heights, to try if the enemy will be so kind as to come out to us." General Washington continued, "The work of constructing the fortifications was commenced about eight o'clock, on the night of the 4th of March, and when morning dawned, the works were in a condition to afford a good defense against small arms and grape shot. The works commanded both the harbor and the town, and left the British but one alternative, either to evacuate the town, or to drive the Americans from their fortifications. The latter course was determined upon, and twenty-four hundred men

were ordered to rendezvous at Castle William, for the purpose of making a night attack upon the works."[1]

The siege guns were now pointing at the British. General William Howe, British Commander-in-Chief and military governor of Massachusetts, had every intention to assault the American positions on Dorchester Heights. However, a violent storm forced the British to cancel their attack. All of Howe's small transport boats were destroyed. The British decided to abandon the city and quickly started loading up their ships in Boston Harbor. The evacuation of Boston had begun. An unwritten truce was called between General Washington and General Howe. The British would not raze the city and the Americans would let the British sail away to Canada and not fire upon them.

Colonel Henry Knox played a major role for the United States in the eight years of fighting the American

⋆ 1 ⋆ HENRY KNOX

Revolution. His first victory was the British surrender of his home town, Boston, Massachusetts. His efforts, along with his men of the "noble train of artillery," secured the first free land for the American cause. The British never returned to Massachusetts as a fighting force during the war.

Henry Knox would soon be awarded a generalship in the Continental Army. Knox then rejoined General Washington in New York. Knox and his men participated in the Battles of Long Island, Trenton, and Princeton, New Jersey. Knox also commanded the siege guns in the ultimate and final victory at the Battle of Yorktown, Virginia in 1781.

Henry Knox founded the Springfield arsenal, in western Massachusetts. He became a major general in 1782. Major General Henry Knox succeeded General Washington as American Commander-in-Chief in late 1783. Knox was the first officer that Washington received at Fraunces Tavern, after Washington's farewell speech to his men. Knox served as the Secretary of War of the United States, from 1785 to 1794. He died in 1806, father of the American artillery.

BENJAMIN TALLMADGE – AMERICA'S FIRST SPY MASTER

Benjamin Tallmadge was one of General George Washington's bright young officers. In 1766, when he was only twelve years old, he was accepted to Yale University. However, his father postponed his university studies until he was fifteen. In 1776, at the age of twenty two, Tallmadge was commissioned a first lieutenant in a Connecticut brigade. He then marched to New York to join General Washington. It was in and around New York City that Tallmadge put his considerable talents to good use for his fledgling nation. He became America's first spy master.

Tallmadge commanded a regiment of dragoons. Dragoons were fast-moving, horseback-riding soldiers. They would scout out British movements and gather military intelligence ahead of the advancing American Army. Working directly under General Charles Scott, Tallmadge recruited patriots who could move with ease behind the enemy lines. Tallmadge established a cryptographical system of messages for his spies. Tallmadge's

cryptographical system included a series of coded words, letters, and invisible ink. Tallmadge and his spy ring used this system for secret communications. After his superior General Scott had to go home on leave, Tallmadge started to report directly to General Washington. The Commander-in-Chief then noticed in the young officer all the honor, leadership, and drive that he expected from all his men.

In 1778, the British Army was camped in New York City where Tallmadge ran one of his espionage operations, known as the Culper Net. Tallmadge had spies who would gather military intelligence by means of dead drop communications. This method of communication involved leaving coded messages hidden in secret places for another American spy to retrieve. Through Tallmadge's spies, pertinent military information reached General Washington's headquarters. For

Benjamin Tallmadge

Set up espionage operation known as the Culper Net in New York City.

2 BENJAMIN TALLMADGE

several years, the Culper Net continued its activity and was very successful. The spy ring had prevented a British plan to attack the French allies in Rhode Island in 1780.

In the fall of 1780, Tallmadge made another contribution to the cause of American independence. Tallmadge discovered General Benedict Arnold's treachery.

The discovery began with the capture of British Major John Andre. Andre was the head of British intelligence in New York City. Andre was masquerading as John Anderson. He was in civilian clothing when captured by three "highway men" sympathetic to the American cause. Andre was caught with notes and sketches of West Point. They were written by Arnold. Arnold wanted to instruct the British on how he would surrender the fort. Arnold wanted to defect for six thousand British pounds and a general's commission. As events unfolded, it was Tallmadge who

first proposed to arrest Arnold, as soon as Andre had confessed. Tallmadge was one of the few American officers who knew of the capture of Andre and of Arnold's deception. Tallmadge would have been able to apprehend Arnold if an unsuspecting Lt. Colonel John Jameson had not inadvertently sent Andre to Arnold while Andre was under arrest. Arnold then slipped away to the enemy. However, this unsuccessful plot to surrender West Point had uncovered other British operatives and spies in New York City. Eventually these people were rounded up and imprisoned by the Americans.

When Tallmadge was not organizing his spy rings, his experience and skill as a dragoon leader led to the defeat and capture of British forts. His lightning-quick raids captured a Tory garrison at Lloyd's Neck on Long Island. It was manned by five hundred loyalists. The capture of Fort George, which had a large quantity of military

provisions, also proved quite successful. After these attacks, General Washington wrote a personal letter of congratulations to Tallmadge. The Congress also recognized Tallmadge.

Tallmadge also contributed to American independence by participating at the Battles of White Plains, Brandywine, Germantown, and Monmouth. Tallmadge's contributions to American independence are quite substantial.

At the end of the war in 1783, Tallmadge retired as a lt. colonel. He became a partner in a general store in his home state of Connecticut. He was also a land speculator. He was elected to Congress in 1800, from Connecticut. Tallmadge lived a long life and died in 1835. The town of Tallmadge, Ohio and the San Diego, California neighborhood Tallmadge were both named in honor of this American Revolutionary War hero.

3

BARON FRIEDRICK WILHELM VON STEUBEN-PRUSSIAN DRILL MASTER

In 1747, Baron Friedrick Wilhelm von Steuben was a seventeen-year-old Prussian officer. He served in the Prussian Army until he was thirty three. In 1763, he was discharged for unknown reasons. von Steuben retired into private life and worked as a chamberlain at the court of Hohenzollern-Hechingen. von Steuben gained the title of Baron at this court. He then immigrated to France in 1771 and attempted unsuccessfully to gain an officer's commission in several European armies.

By 1777, von Steuben's military reputation had led him to the attention of Benjamin Franklin. Franklin was then in Paris as America's representative to the French crown. On Franklin's recommendation, the former Prussian officer eventually made his way to the United States that year. von Steuben carried with him documents that promised him a Continental Army officer's commission. Franklin had written a letter to General George Washington introducing von

Steuben as a former lt. general in the King of Prussia's army. Actually, von Steuben was no more than a captain in Frederick the Great's army; however, von Steuben knew how to train military troops, and this is what the American Army needed in the winter of 1777-1778. Congress commissioned him a major general and appointed him Inspector General of the army on the recommendation of General Washington.

When von Steuben joined the American Army, he immediately ordered that the men be trained by officers and not sergeants. He knew that this was the quickest and easiest way to build discipline and professionalism in the American camp at Valley Forge. von Steuben believed that the men needed to have more direct contact with their officers and that the officers needed to work on their commands to the troops. The

Baron von Steuben

He wrote the American Army's first training manual and he "professionalized" the army.

3 BARON FRIEDRICK WILHELM VON STEUBEN

Prussian initially trained a small core of approximately one hundred men. Soon, all the soldiers were striving to be like the chosen one hundred. During the pitiful winter encampment at Valley Forge, the Baron managed to mold the whole American Army into a viable fighting force. von Steuben wrote the American Army's first training manual, called "Regulations for the Order and Discipline of the Troops of the United States." This manual was commonly known as the "Blue Book." von Steuben spoke no English; the book's translation was written by Lt. Colonel Alexander Hamilton, then an aide-de-camp to General Washington. At times, von Steuben must have seemed comical to the troops. When the troops did not perform up to his standards, he would curse them in German, then French, and if that did not work, he would have an aide curse them in English.

Major General von Steuben's experience and leadership changed the American Army from a "rag-tag" mix of regulars and colonial militiamen into a professional army capable of resisting the most powerful army on earth. Without von Steuben's training, the American Army surely would have suffered heavy losses at the Battle of Barren Hill. But because von Steuben trained them well, the American Army narrowly escaped a crushing defeat and made an orderly retreat. von Steuben's transformation of the American Army was an extraordinary achievement.

Shortly after the Battle of Barren Hill, the Americans fought the British to a draw at the Battle of Monmouth, New Jersey. von Steuben was first to realize that the British were heading for Monmouth, and his leadership helped steady the American Army during the battle. General Washington and Lt. Colonel Alexander Hamilton also fought at that battle.

General Washington had full confidence in von Steuben as he became the Commander-in-Chief's representative to Congress in 1779.

When the Southern campaigns of the war were underway in the Carolinas, Georgia, and Virginia, von Steuben was still fighting alongside General Washington. At the last great battle of the American Revolutionary War, the Battle of Yorktown, Virginia, von Steuben was appointed a division commander. He witnessed the surrender of British Commander Lord Charles Cornwallis and the grand British Army in October 1781.

Major General Baron von Steuben helped in the demobilization of the American Army after the war. He then retired to New York State. A grateful New York gave von Steuben, 16,000 acres of land. This land was secured with the help of his good friend, Alexander Hamilton.

Major General Baron von Steuben was the first professional "drill master" and teacher

⋆ 3 ⋆ BARON FRIEDRICK WILHELM VON STEUBEN

of the young American Army. He is the man most responsible for its inception into professionalism. von Steuben died in 1794 an American citizen and Revolutionary War hero.

JAMES MONROE-HERO FROM VIRGINIA

The American Revolution erupted in 1775. The boy who was to become the fifth President of the United States was a seventeen-year-old student at William and Mary College in Virginia. By September 1775, the young James Monroe had gained an officer's commission as a second lieutenant in the third Virginia volunteers.

Monroe admired Lt. Colonel Thomas Knowlton's heroism at the Battle of Bunker Hill. So the young Monroe volunteered to fight under Knowlton's command at the Battle of Harlem Heights in September 1776. When Knowlton was killed in action, Monroe was suddenly thrust into a commanding position.

At the Battle of Trenton in December 1776, Monroe was partnered with General Washington's cousin Captain William Washington for a special mission. Monroe and William Washington attacked and captured the enemy Hessian cannon. Unfortunately, Monroe was seriously wounded. But Monroe's heroism played an essential role in the surprise American victory. Under the command of Captain Alexander Hamilton, the Americans won the day at Trenton.

Monroe gallantly saw action in the battles of Brandywine, Germantown, and Monmouth. He served as a staff officer to the American Commander-in-Chief General George Washington and spent the cold miserable winter of 1777-1778 at Valley Forge.

Monroe was only twenty years old when he resigned his military commission in November 1778 and moved back to his home state of Virginia. But in a little more than three years, Monroe had attained the prominent rank of lt. colonel.

Back in Virginia, Thomas Jefferson (the man who would become the third President of the United States) took an interest in

James Monroe

He was severely wounded during the Battle of Trenton. He later became the fifth President of the United States in 1816.

★ ★ ★
★ 4 ★ JAMES MONROE
★ ★ ★ ★

young James Monroe. Under Jefferson's guidance, Monroe studied law and politics and became Governor of Virginia. He also served as a United States Senator from Virginia from 1790 to 1794. Monroe served with the Virginia Assembly that ratified the Federal Constitution. While in France in 1803, Monroe helped negotiate the purchase of the Louisiana territory. Monroe later served as Secretary of State during the War of 1812. He also served as the Secretary of War in 1814-1815.

James Monroe became the fifth President of the United Sates in 1816. Monroe served two terms. He retired to Virginia in 1825 and died in 1831.

James Monroe was a very accomplished Revolutionary War hero. Monroe served the United States for fifty years of his life. He is famous for his Monroe Doctrine. This doctrine warned all European powers to steer clear of any territorial designs on any part of the Western Hemisphere.

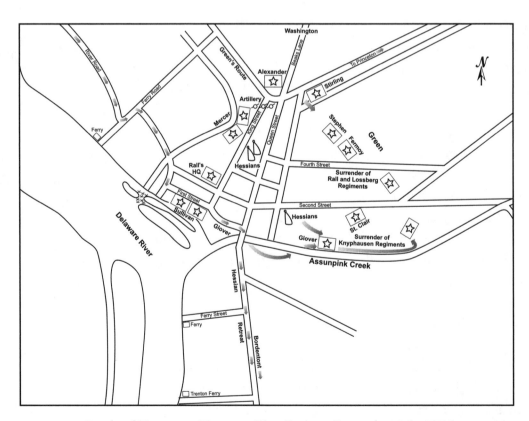

Battle of Trenton – Trenton, New Jersey – December 26, 1776

NATHANAEL GREEN – THE RIGHT CHOICE

There isn't an American general during the American Revolutionary War that surpasses Nathanael Green in leadership abilities. General George Washington grew to depend upon Green's many talents. At the Battle of Bunker Hill, Green lifted the spirits of the young American Army with the idea that the battle was actually a tactical victory and not a defeat. Green said, "I hope we can offer them another battle at a similar price." Although the British had gained Bunker Hill and the Charlestown peninsula, they suffered many casualties. Nearly, 1,100 British "redcoats" were either killed or wounded at the grand battle. During the Battle of Bunker Hill, Green was in command of three regiments at nearby Prospect Hill, only a few miles west of Charlestown, and did not actively participate in the fighting.

Green was born in Warwick, Rhode Island in 1742. He was from a Quaker family and was the son of an anchor smith. As a young boy, Green trained in his father's trade. However, he also had a love for books. Green collected books, especially books about military history. As a boy, he was a very good student and he learned to read and write Latin. But it was clear that his passion was anything to do with military study. This passion would unfortunately cost him his membership in his religious community. Subsequently, the Quakers, who do not believe in warfare, disowned Green.

As a young man, Green's political capabilities enabled him to serve as a representative in the Rhode Island Legislature. In 1774, Green helped organize a militia unit. He enlisted as a private. However, it was clear to everyone that Green was a leader among men. When news came of the Battles of Lexington and Concord,

Nathanael Green

Commanded American troops in the Southern campaign. He is recognized as the most competent American general during the American Revolution.

★ 5 ★ NATHANAEL GREEN

young Nathanael volunteered his services, and he traveled north with his militia unit to the patriot camp in Cambridge, Massachusetts. At Cambridge, without any high-ranking officer from his town to take command, Green was voted a brigadier general by the townsmen to the Rhode Island militia. Green was humbled by his appointment, and at age thirty three he was the youngest general in the Rhode Island militia. During the siege of Boston, Green showed all the talents necessary to become a general, as he helped organize supplies for the American Army. Within a few months, Green was offered a commission in the Continental Army, as a brigadier general. Again, Green was the youngest man who received a brigadier generalship from Congress.

Commander-in-Chief General George Washington understood the value that Green brought to the American Army. Green's organizational skills were highly valued by the

Commander-in-Chief. Shortly after the Battle of Long Island, in August of 1776, Green was promoted by Congress to major general at the insistence of General Washington. Green's promotion by Congress in this two-year period was a meteoric rise for a man who was originally just a private in the Rhode Island militia.

Major General Green had a clear understanding of the logistics of supplying an army. Because of this understanding, he was appointed Quartermaster General by Congress during the cold, long winter at Valley Forge in 1777-1778. Green's job was almost impossible to undertake, but, he did his job well. The Congress had no money and supplies were hard to find. Green pleaded with Congress for funds to buy supplies. Green organized "foraging parties" that would scour the countryside for food. The soldiers would often resort to stealing what they could not buy. Green did the best he could during these trying con-

ditions. He improved the transportation of supplies and developed a system of field depots where supplies were stored. Green was Quartermaster General until 1780.

Major General Green possessed other valuable talents that made him indispensable to the American cause. He was a master at understanding the topography of the land and of reading maps. He understood how and where to place troops within the confines of the land. These talents were very important in the Revolutionary War, as armies tried to out-maneuver each other in often unfamiliar land. Travel was slow. Reaching a destination before the enemy was paramount. Often deployed advantageously on the high ground, Green prepared his men for battle.

Major General Green commanded brigades during the losses at the Battles of Brandywine and Germantown. At Brandywine, Green managed to stop a British advance, one of the lone bright efforts by

★ 5 ★ NATHANAEL GREEN

an American commander. And at the Battle of Monmouth, he led the right column of command that was instrumental in the morale-building victory. The Battle of Monmouth was the last major battle of the war in the north. Although Monmouth was considered a draw, it was the best effort that the American Army had yet produced. The Americans showed courage and the officers portrayed fine leadership abilities.

Nathanael Green was also an excellent diplomat for the United States. Green used these skills after the Battle of Newport, Rhode Island in the summer of 1778. Dispatched to Boston with the Marquis de Lafayette, Green stopped a growing rift between the Americans and their French allies. A lack of cooperation existed between General John Sullivan and French Admiral Charles d'Estaing. Admiral d'Estaing had refused to land French troops at Sullivan's demand in Rhode Island. d'Estaing sailed to Boston,

where he met Lafayette and Green. In Boston, these tensions were quelled with a series of meetings explaining what was expected from both allied forces.

When the war headed to the southern states, the Commander-in-Chief's first and only choice as a commanding general was Major General Green. The Southern campaign is where Green helped turn the war in America's favor. Three previous commanders of the important southern department had failed spectacularly. Green's simple strategy was to divide his army. When he did this, he effectively created several small armies that harassed British Commander-in-Chief Lord Cornwallis' Army. Green curtailed the operations of the "terror of the South," Major Banastre Tarleton. Green made the right choice in dispatching Brigadier General Daniel Morgan to face Tarleton at the Battle of Cowpens. In early 1781, Morgan defeated Tarleton. The final American

victory in the War of Independence was only several months away, at Yorktown.

Major General Green was simply the most effective and competent American general during the Revolutionary War. General Washington always made the right choice when appointing Green to a command, for Green almost always made the right choice in his command. An American Revolutionary War hero, Green died of sun-stroke at the age of forty four, in Georgia in 1786.

MARQUIS DE LAFAYETTE – BOY GENERAL FROM FRANCE

The year was 1769. Twelve-year-old Marquis de Lafayette was orphaned. Luckily for Lafayette he was a French nobleman from a wealthy aristocratic family.

At age fourteen in 1771, Lafayette joined the French Army. It was not uncommon for boys as young as fourteen to join the military during the eighteenth century. Four years later, when the American Revolutionary War started, he was drawn to the ideals that America was offering the world. Lafayette was impressed by American ideals of liberty and democracy. The pursuit of liberty and democracy became his personal chase.

When he was nineteen-years-old, the Marquis de Lafayette sought an officer's commission in the Continental Army. He wanted to fight for America. Lafayette had told American diplomats in Paris that he didn't need or want to be paid. He just wanted to serve liberty's cause as a volunteer. Lafayette's persistence was rewarded when he left for America with the promise that he would become a major general in the Continental Army.

When the French teenager arrived at General Washington's headquarters, the Commander-in-Chief didn't exactly know what to do with the idealistic young man. Lafayette had never seen military action, yet he desired a field command. He had the promise that he would become an American general. General Washington had a decision to make. Would the Commander-in-Chief risk the lives of American soldiers and maybe the fate of the nation for an untested young man's dreams?

Soon, circumstances quickly led to General Washington's confidence in Lafayette. Lafayette served with distinction in battle and was wounded at the Battle of Brandywine. At Brandywine, Lafayette and his men held off a British advance.

Marquis de Lafayette

The American Revolution inspired the idealized French nobleman. He faithfully served General Washington as a field commander and diplomat.

★ 6 ★ MARQUIS DE LAFAYETTE

Within six months of arriving in America and joining the Continental Army, Lafayette had gained his wish with the command of a division. Shortly afterward, Congress approved his commission as a major general. Lafayette was now the proud leader of Virginian troops. Lafayette was also a military veteran after having seen action at Brandywine and Glouster, New Jersey.

At the winter camp at Valley Forge, Lafayette joined General Washington's staff. Their relationship quickly blossomed. General Washington had no children, and Lafayette looked upon General Washington as a father figure.

During encampment at Valley Forge, a group of officers attempted to have General Washington removed as the Commander-in-Chief. A secret scheme was plotted against General Washington. Lafayette, however, remained loyal to his father figure. This plot is known as the Conway Cabal. This cabal is incorrectly named

after Major General Thomas Conway of New Jersey. Conway was only having a disagreement with General Washington about how Conway was to receive his new duties and was not part of the scheme to remove General Washington. This attempt to remove General Washington was led by some of the New England members of Congress and some military officers. The Congressional New Englanders felt they had lost a significant leadership role in the revolution. They were also questioning General Washington's leadership ability. The army had suffered some terrible disasters under his leadership. However, General Washington persevered this trying time at Valley Forge. General Washington always held the support of Lafayette and other like-minded officers.

Major General Lafayette had also shown considerable political skills. He was hand-picked by General Horatio Gates to lead an invasion of Canada. Gates at the time was

a rival to General Washington. This proposed invasion, if undertaken, would have been a disaster for the Americans. The current American Army in upstate New York had insufficient supplies to undertake such a major operation. After arriving in Albany, New York and reviewing the troops, Lafayette sent a letter to General Washington informing him of the folly of invading Canada. Congress in turn acknowledged the plight of the army and correctly cancelled the ill-fated plans.

After the frustrating experience in New York, Lafayette returned to Valley Forge in the spring of 1778. He then took part in the action at Barren Hill. At the Battle of Monmouth, Lafayette again received the accolades of General Washington because of his leadership skills. The young general from France was now fulfilling his dreams of command and also meeting the needs of the Continental Army with his outstanding leadership.

6 ★ MARQUIS DE LAFAYETTE

During the Battle of Newport, Rhode Island, General Washington gave Lafayette the command of two brigades. Meanwhile, Lafayette helped ease the growing tensions between his French countrymen and the Americans with his diplomatic skills. Lafayette was dispatched to Boston from Newport to talk to French Admiral Charles d'Estaing, about his growing rift with American General Sullivan.

During the war Lafayette had traveled back to France and successfully persuaded the French foreign minister, Charles Vergennes, to send an expeditionary force to America. On his return to the United States in 1780, Lafayette again took command of Virginian troops. He fought and harassed British Commander Lord Cornwallis during the Southern Campaigns. Finally by 1781,

with the French navy and General Washington both moving to the south, Lafayette was given command of a division during the final battle of the revolution at Yorktown.

After Yorktown and the defeat of the British in America, Lafayette returned to France as a hero. He carried with him a letter of praise and appreciation from General Washington. In this letter, General Washington said, "I owe it to your friendship and to my affectionate regard for you, my dear Marquis. I do not want you to leave this country without carrying with you fresh marks of my deepest attachment to you and of the new expressions and the high sense I entertain of your military conduct and other important services in the last campaign at Yorktown, although the latter are too well known to need any testimony of my approbation."

The Marquis de Lafayette twice returned to the United States after the war, once in 1784 at the request of George Washington and later in 1825. In 1825 he toured the nation, making stops in most of the major cities. Lafayette helped dedicate the Bunker Hill Monument in Charlestown, Massachusetts on June 17, 1825, the 50th anniversary of the legendary battle.

During the war Lafayette had spent $200,000 of his own fortune in support of American independence. Although a Frenchman, Lafayette is fondly remembered as an American hero. He was buried in France in 1834, with some American soil that he had brought back with him.

Viva Marie Joseph Paul Yves Roch Gilbert du Montier, the Marquis de Lafayette.

DANIEL STOCKWELL JR. – MASSACHUSETTS MINUTEMAN

Daniel Stockwell Jr. was a thirty-year-old farmer from Westboro, Massachusetts when the "shot heard around the world" was fired on the Lexington green. It was April 19, 1775. Born in 1744, Stockwell was called out to the alarm on that day. That fateful evening he found himself at the American camp. He was with his brothers and cousins. They were minutemen. A minuteman was ready to fight on a moment's notice. The Stockwell men were enlisted in the Massachusetts militia. They converged upon the green of Harvard University at Cambridge, Massachusetts, where the Americans had set up their military camp.

Events were moving quickly as American patriots rushed in from all around New England. The small New England Army surrounded the peninsular town of Boston, where the British had their army. A showdown was in the making.

Stockwell was the father of four children. He wasn't substantially different from any other minuteman who answered the call to arms. He was simply an American patriot willing to sacrifice everything dear to him and everything that was dear to his family for the love of liberty and country.

The American commanding officers in Cambridge were planning military strategies to defeat the British. For almost two months following the gunfire at Lexington and Concord and the battle road back to Boston, the Americans argued their strategies. They had surrounded the town of Boston. How could they run the British out of Boston? They decided to build fortifications in Charlestown, directly opposite Boston. The two towns are separated by the Charles River, less than one mile apart. So on the night of June 16, 1775, 1,200 Americans built a redoubt on Breeds Hill in Charlestown.

Daniel Stockwell Jr.

Returned with Henry Knox from Ft. Ticonderoga to Boston with artillery. He later helped fortify Dorchester Heights overlooking Boston.

★ 7 ★ DANIEL STOCKWELL JR.

Breeds Hill is only one half mile south of Bunker Hill.

The first great battle of the American Revolution took place the next day, June 17, 1775. Although most of the fighting took place on Breeds Hill, the battle is remembered as the legendary Battle of Bunker Hill. This legendary battle showed the British that the Americans could and would face off against them in mortal combat. The British Army was considered the best army in the world because of their leadership, armaments, and tactics. Their professional army was simply second to none. The British did not think that a "rag-tag" army of colonials would be able to stand up to them. The British were wrong. The Americans were excellent marksmen. They were able to rapid-fire their muskets as quickly and lethally as any professional soldier. The American patriots aimed to shelter and protect themselves during battle. They successfully did this with their small earthen

redoubt fort that they built on Breeds Hill. This tactic worked. Although the British gained a territorial victory, the Americans inflicted over one thousand casualties on the King's men. The British casualties at the Battle of Bunker Hill had impaired the manner in which they employed their tactics and strategies during the next eight long years of fighting, eventually helping the Americans win the struggle for independence.

On June 15, 1775, two days before the Battle of Bunker Hill, the Continental Congress chose Colonel George Washington of Virginia as the Commander-in-Chief of the American Army. He immediately set off from Philadelphia to Cambridge to take command of the American troops. On his way to Cambridge a messenger informed him of the great battle.

General Washington was soon reviewing his troops and meeting his officers and men, including Daniel Stockwell Jr.

Stockwell was a sergeant and a natural leader who had never met anybody from Virginia before. Stockwell was certainly impressed with the tall American Commander-in-Chief. Stockwell had heard about General Washington from his father, Daniel Sr., and Timothy Warren, his father-in-law. Like General Washington, Daniel Sr. and Warren had fought with the British against the French, during the French and Indian War, fifteen years earlier.

General Washington faced a lot of work trying to transform his "rag-tag" army of New England farmers and tradesmen into a viable fighting force. General Washington needed a lot of help. One of the men that General Washington grew to rely upon was Sergeant Stockwell.

Sergeant Stockwell volunteered to travel with Colonel Henry Knox to Fort Ticonderoga in northern New York. Knox had been ordered to retrieve fifty nine cannons and

7 DANIEL STOCKWELL JR.

mortars that were to be placed around Boston and on Dorchester Heights during the siege of the town. Knox and Stockwell made the grueling 650 mile roundtrip in midwinter—the very cold and snowy winter of 1775-1776. This "noble train of artillery" accomplished its mission and placed the large siege guns facing the British forces occupying Boston.

On the horizon, a great battle was shaping up. General Washington was making plans with his staff officers to defeat the British. The British, meanwhile, were making plans of their own to finally crush the rebels of New England. What the British didn't know was that on the night of March 4, 1776, Sergeant Stockwell and the artillery men of the American Army had built a series of small redoubts on Dorchester Heights. The Americans then pointed their siege guns toward Boston and General Howe's British Army. Amazed at the sight of the American cannons pointing at them, General Howe wisely conceded the town of Boston to the American Army. When a large winter storm tore through Boston, Howe realized it was time to evacuate the town. British morale was low and all of Howe's transport boats were destroyed. These events had convinced Howe of the folly of another bloody battle.

On March 17, 1776, the British sailed to Canada. General George Washington and Sergeant Daniel Stockwell Jr., along with nine thousand other American patriots, forced the grand British Army to surrender the town of Boston and the Colony of Massachusetts. The British never returned to Massachusetts as a fighting force during the American Revolutionary War. Eight more years of warfare would be played out in every other American state, until the surrender of General Lord Cornwallis at Yorktown, Virginia, on October 19, 1781. The Yorktown victory assured American independence from Britain.

Sergeant Daniel Stockwell Jr. retired to Royalston, Massachusetts in 1790, with his wife, Rebecca, and eleven children. He died in Royalston in 1817.[1] He was an American Revolutionary War Hero.

ISRAEL PUTNAM – OLD YANKEE GENERAL

A t the onset of the American Revolutionary War, Israel Putnam was already a crusty old war veteran, much older than most of his fellow patriots. His men affectionately called him "Old Put." Putnam was born in Massachusetts in 1718. Putnam moved with his family to Connecticut in 1740.

In the French and Indian War of 1756-1763, Britain and France fought for the control of Canada. Putnam joined Robert's Rangers, the famous colonial militia battalion in which Putnam learned the art of warfare. In the French and Indian War, most Native Americans sided with the French against the British and Americans. Putnam experienced the Indian threat firsthand. He was captured and narrowly escaped being burned at the stake.

When the "shot heard around the world" was fired at Lexington, Massachusetts on April 19, 1775, Putnam was reportedly plowing his fields. He unhitched one of his strongest horses and immediately rode one hundred miles north to the American camp at Cambridge, Massachusetts. Old Put was reporting for duty. At Cambridge he was promoted from colonel to brigadier general in the Connecticut militia. Before the Battle of Bunker Hill, Putnam was given command of the Connecticut third regiment.

During the evening of June 15, 1775, Putnam was at a war council. He was with the Commander-in-Chief of the American Army, General Artemus Ward, of Massachusetts. All of the other colonial leaders of the Committee of Safety were also present. They decided to fortify and defend the prominent hill of Charlestown. This hill was called Bunker Hill.

The next night, Putnam had wagons filled with picks, axes, and shovels. That evening twelve hundred Americans built a redoubt or small earthen fort, facing south toward Boston. Putnam knew that

Israel Putnam

He helped command American forces at the Battle of Bunker Hill.

✶ 8 ✶ ISRAEL PUTNAM

the Americans would fight to the death if they had fortifications for their protection.

This small redoubt amazed and shocked the British when they first saw it at the break of dawn. The Americans had actually built their redoubt on nearby Breeds Hill. Whether by design or mistake, the Americans had chosen the smaller but closer hill overlooking Boston. The British made no mistake about the "invitation" to come and fight. The British were more than happy to accommodate the rebels.

The British mustered their troops. They crossed the Charles River in small transport boats. It was a hot summer day. Ten hours passed since the British awoke to the sight of the American fortifications on Breeds Hill. The grand Battle of Bunker Hill began at three o'clock. As the battle commenced, General Putnam was seemingly everywhere at once. He was riding his horse urging the men to fight. Putnam is sometimes credited, along with

Colonel William Prescott, as giving the famous order: "Don't fire until you see the whites of their eyes."

The British made three courageous but very costly attacks upon the small redoubt. They lost nearly a quarter of all the officers that would become casualties in the eight years of fighting. British casualties numbered 1,054 men, 226 were killed, and 828 were wounded, amounting to almost half of their army! Even more appalling were the casualties to their officers: ninety two killed or wounded, out of 250 officers. American casualties were also heavy; they suffered 140 dead, while 271 were listed as wounded and thirty listed as captured.

The British captured the redoubt and the peninsula of Charlestown. Although the Battle of Bunker Hill was a territorial victory for the British, the Americans inflicted heavy losses on the King's army. So American morale did not suffer, the American officers realized

they knew the enemy and could predict his strategies. Not long before, in the French and Indian War, the British themselves had given the Americans military training and experience. The Americans now understood that they could stand up to the greatest army in the world. This costly victory for the British hindered the manner in which they fought the rest of the war.

General Israel Putnam played a large part in this effort. His efforts to rally the men at Bunker Hill were heroic. A few weeks after the Battle of Bunker Hill, General George Washington took command of the American Army in Cambridge. General Washington met the men who would guide and lead the patriot troops during the successful siege of Boston. Many of these officers and men would be with General Washington during the eight years of fighting for independence. They became the nucleus of the Continental Army. Putnam, now a major

8 ISRAEL PUTNAM

general in the Continental Army, would not be one of them. Putnam unfortunately had a debilitating stroke in late 1779.

But while Putnam was still able-bodied, he stayed in the fight. After the British evacuated Boston, Major General Putnam was ordered to New York to relieve General Sullivan as commander of some troops. However, Putnam failed to beat back the advances of British Commander-in-Chief, General Howe. American leadership failed at the Battle of Long Island. Retreat and evacuation

ruled the day for the patriot cause. More importantly, however, the American patriot army survived. They were able to regroup to fight another day.

Major General Putnam was now nearly sixty years old. He held several other commands, at Philadelphia, Pennsylvania; Princeton, New Jersey; Redding, Connecticut; and Norwalk, Connecticut. He returned home and recruited more New England troops for the Continental Army. In May 1779, he returned to New York to lead American forces along the Hudson River until his

stroke in December of that year.

Major General Israel Putnam is best remembered as the fearless leader at the Battle of Bunker Hill. As a general, Putnam sought out the enemy to destroy the enemy. Sometimes he was successful and other times he was not. However, Putnam's valor and fearless courage enabled him to fight and lead his patriot men for the liberty of America and these are the reasons he is an American Revolutionary War hero. He died in 1790.

9

JOHN STARK – "LIVE FREE OR DIE"

John Stark gave the state of New Hampshire its motto "Live Free or Die." Stark was an experienced military man when the Revolutionary War started in Massachusetts on April 19, 1775. When Stark heard of the battles at Lexington and Concord, he immediately left his farm and rode to Cambridge, Massachusetts.

John Stark was a colonel in the New Hampshire militia. At the American camp in Cambridge, he organized the New Hampshire minutemen into a regiment. This regiment distinguished itself at the Battle of Bunker Hill on June 17, 1775.

When the Battle of Bunker Hill began, Stark and his men were protecting the town of Cambridge. Meanwhile, General Israel Putnam of Connecticut was at American headquarters asking for more troops to enter into the battle. Putnam was pleading with General Artemus Ward, the Commander-in-Chief of American forces, to order Stark's men into the battle. General Ward finally agreed with Putnam and sent Stark and his New Hampshire sharp shooters to Charlestown. When Stark reached Bunker Hill he noticed that the American left flank was open to British advances, along the Mystic River beach. Stark ordered his men to build a rail fence on the beach for protection. This rail fence began along the eight-foot-high bluffs to the river's edge; it was twelve feet wide. On the beach, Stark and his marksmen made a stand and inflicted heavy casualties on British Commander General Howe's light infantry. Ninety six British regulars fell dead in front of this rail fence barricade. While reviewing the carnage on the beach, Stark commented that the scores of the British dead were akin to sheep lying thickly in their fold. Indeed, British soldiers did lie dead upon each other, as wave after wave of British regulars

John Stark
Commanded troops at Bunker Hill, Bennington and Saratoga. He is credited with the motto: "Live Free or Die".

★ 9 ★ JOHN STARK

marched directly into the musket fire of the New Hampshire marksmen. The Battle of Bunker Hill continued for two more hours, until the patriots finally ran out of gunpowder. The patriots then managed an orderly retreat back to the safety of Cambridge.

After the siege of Boston was over, General Washington ordered Stark to accompany him to New Jersey. Stark took part in the Battle of Trenton on December 26, 1776. In this early American victory, Stark commanded the right column of American forces.

Colonel Stark and his New Hampshire men next engaged the enemy at Bennington, Vermont in August 1777. Stark had raised fifteen hundred men, many of them veterans of the Battle of Bunker Hill. At Bennington, Colonel Stark and Captain Seth Warner of Vermont killed, wounded, or captured nearly one thousand enemy troops. The American victory at Bennington depleted British General "Gentleman" Johnny Burgoyne's army. By mid-October of 1777, General Stark had also successfully cut off a possible escape route of Burgoyne's army. Stark's efforts forced Burgoyne to surrender after only one week of fighting in the Battle of Saratoga. General Horatio Gates, the American commander, accepted the British surrender. As a reward for his outstanding leadership at Bennington, Congress promoted Stark to the rank of brigadier general in the Continental Army.

General John Stark was at the right place at the right time for the new nation. Through Stark's efforts, Americans gained independence from Britain. At the Battles of Bunker Hill, Bennington, and Saratoga, Stark provided the leadership that the Americans needed. Stark twice commanded the Northern War Department and served in Rhode Island, in 1779. He later returned to command troops in New Jersey in 1780.

John Stark became a major general on September 30, 1783, and retired from the army on November 3, 1783. He returned home and stayed out of public life for the remainder of his days. He died in New Hampshire in 1822, at the age of ninety three. Today, Stark remains not only an icon to the people of New Hampshire, but also an American Revolutionary War hero.

10

JOHN SULLIVAN – LAWYER FROM NEW HAMPSHIRE

Some historians argue that the American Revolution really started in 1774. The British controlled Fort William and Mary, strategically located in Portsmouth, New Hampshire. In a bold and daring military action, Major John Sullivan, a lawyer and member of the First Continental Congress, led a successful raid upon the fort. This attack enabled the New Hampshire militia to secure the strategic location and to capture much-needed gunpowder. Sullivan's military action preceded the battles of Lexington and Concord by one year.

After the Battle of Bunker Hill on June 17, 1775, Sullivan received one of the first commissions as a brigadier general in the Continental Army. During the siege of Boston, Sullivan commanded a brigade that protected Plowed Hill. He was with General George Washington when American troops entered Boston after the British surrendered and evacuated the town on March 17, 1776.

After the British left Boston, the Commander-in-Chief ordered Sullivan to reinforce the invasion troops heading for Canada. Sullivan marched north with his orders. He took command of the American Army in northern New York. Smallpox had raged among the American troops; the previous commander, General John Thomas, had died of the disease. The army was in disarray, so Sullivan ordered a retreat. Congress criticized him, but historians agree Sullivan had assessed the military situation correctly. He was appointed a major general in August of 1776.

Major General Sullivan received orders to travel to New York City and rejoin General Washington. In New York, he was given command of Long Island, but General Washington overrode those orders after only four days. General Washington gave the

John Sullivan

Captured Fort William and Mary in Portsmouth, New Hampshire in 1774.

⁑ 10 ⁑ JOHN SULLIVAN

command of Long Island to General Israel Putnam. Putnam was a more senior officer. During the British attack on Long Island, Sullivan was captured and taken to Philadelphia. He was then, however, pardoned and soon exchanged for a British General.

Major General Sullivan rejoined General Washington in New Jersey. He was with the American Army when General Washington crossed the Delaware River on Christmas evening 1776. The Battle of Trenton occurred the next day. Sullivan's division captured a key bridge, preventing the escape of Hessian mercenaries and thus ensuring the surprise American victory.

In early 1777, Major General Sullivan helped defeat the British at the Battle of Princeton. He then took part in the Philadelphia campaign. Sullivan continually raided and harassed the British. He was one of the American commanders at the Battle of Brandywine. The Americans lost that battle. No American general showed much tactical leadership in that

loss, but Sullivan became the scapegoat for that American defeat. Congress issued an inquiry into Sullivan's actions and charged him with misconduct. He was facing a court martial. But General Washington came to the defense of his trusted friend. General Washington regarded Sullivan as one of his most valuable commanders, and he knew the charges against Sullivan were false. General Washington demanded that Sullivan retain his command. General Washington got his wish. Sullivan was cleared of all charges of wrongdoing and he led his troops on to Germantown in October of 1777.

Major General Sullivan spent the winter of 1777-1778 with the Commander-in-Chief at Valley Forge. During the joint Franco-American operation in the summer of 1778, Sullivan took command of the troops at Newport, Rhode Island.

Major General Sullivan's last campaign was his expedition against the Iroquois Indian Federation in the spring of

1779. The Iroquois were allies of the British. Sullivan's march on the Iroquois Nation employed an "all-out scorched earth" policy. He ordered his men to burn Iroquois villages to the ground and to destroy all their crops, fruit trees, and animals. The Six Nations of the Iroquois Federation were severely punished for siding with the British. After Sullivan's campaign, they were not a factor in the war.

In the fall of 1779, Major General Sullivan resigned from the Continental Army because of poor health. The Revolutionary War hero returned to New Hampshire and was elected to the Second Continental Congress. Sullivan later served two terms as governor of New Hampshire, from 1785 to 1790. President Washington appointed him a federal judge; that post was his last service to his state and his new nation. Major General John Sullivan died an American Revolutionary War hero in 1795.

ALEXANDER HAMILTON – A HAMILTONIAN AMERICA

After the American Revolution, every free man had the opportunity to rise up socially and economically regardless of his station at the time of his birth. A poor immigrant boy took advantage of this new opportunity in the United States of America. He was from the West Indian island of Nevis. This young man was Alexander Hamilton.

Hamilton was born in 1757 to a French mother and Scottish father. During the American Revolution, Hamilton became one of General George Washington's youngest aide-de-camp officers. He wrote letters for General Washington and passed on his commands. Hamilton eventually became a "founding father" of the young nation.

Hamilton immigrated to America when he was fifteen years old to attend school at Elizabethtown, New Jersey. In 1773 he attended Kings College, now called Columbia University, in New York. By 1774, young Hamilton was writing political pamphlets. His writing quickly earned him a growing reputation as one of the colonies' most promising young patriots.

At age eighteen, Hamilton was commissioned as a captain in the colonial militia of New York. It was 1776. When hostilities began, he was with an artillery company. Although a young man rarely held a captain's commission, Hamilton's reputation as a leading patriot had earned him this rank. Captain Hamilton met the Commander-in-Chief General George Washington in 1776. After its victory in Boston, the Continental Army marched to New York City. Shortly afterward, Captain Hamilton declined an opportunity to join the officers' staff of General William Alexander. Captain Hamilton instead chose to remain with his artillery company. He was loyal to

Alexander Hamilton
General Washington's aide-de-camp. He wrote the majority of the Federalist Papers and later became first Secretary of the Treasury.

his men, and he desired to see action as an artilleryman.

Captain Hamilton fought at the Battles of Long Island and White Plains. He then distinguished himself at the Battle of Trenton. Hamilton, along with artillery chief General Henry Knox, stopped the advance of the Hessian mercenaries. The Hessians attacked, but were repulsed when a combination of artillery shot and flanking fire silenced them. Hamilton's men charged toward the Hessian position and captured the enemy batteries.

Captain Hamilton also fought at the Battle of Princeton and his gallantry gained the admiration of General Washington. Then, on March 1, 1777, the Commander-in-Chief asked him to become one of his personal secretaries. Hamilton accepted. He was promoted to lt. colonel shortly afterward and served as General Washington's aide-de-camp for five years. Hamilton began to advise General Washington on military strategy.

At Valley Forge, the British almost captured Lt. Colonel Hamilton. Hamilton had orders to guard some provisions at the ruins of an old flour mill. Hamilton followed military procedures. He posted guards to warn of any enemy movement. But in spite of Hamilton's precautions, the British eventually attacked his small unit and drove them out. Hamilton and his men barely escaped.

During the Battle of Yorktown, Virginia, Lt. Colonel Hamilton returned to command a battalion of four hundred men. Hamilton led the attack on the small British earthen fort, named redoubt Number 10. A French battalion attacked redoubt Number 9. This coordinated assault was a complete success. The allies had gained valuable ground. The end of the war had begun for the British. Pressure was mounting for British Commander General Lord Cornwallis to surrender his army. Cornwallis eventually surrendered on October 19, 1781. Hamilton

had shown great leadership, while his courage was second to none, in the final battle of the American Revolution.

While Hamilton was working as General Washington's aide-de-camp he was writing economic programs for the fledgling United States. And just before the Revolutionary War ended, Congress promoted Hamilton to full colonel. The people of New York elected Hamilton to Congress in 1782. He stayed in Congress for only one year and retired to practice law in New York in 1783.

In 1788, Hamilton was a major contributor in the ratification of the United States Constitution. He wrote a majority of the Federalist Papers. The Federalist Papers were written to gain popular support for the ratification of the purposed Constitution. Hamilton's Federalist Papers had argued for a strong central government. Hamilton served at the pleasure of President Washington as the nation's first Secretary of the Treasury from

1789 to 1795. Hamilton successfully implemented his policy of assumption in an effort to not only appear more united as a nation, but to attract future investors and repay existing creditors. With assumption, the Federal Government consolidated all of the Revolutionary War debt incurred by all of the states, including its own debt into interest-bearing bonds. With interest-bearing bonds, investors could expect a profit with the full faith and credit of the United States government.

Alexander Hamilton's death resulted from a pistol duel with then Vice President Aaron Burr, a longtime political foe. Hamilton had always opposed Burr in any election, including campaigns for the governorship of New York, the United States senate, and the presidency. This famous duel was fought because Burr perceived he was again a victim of Hamilton's political hostility. Hamilton had called Burr a dangerous man who was not to be trusted with the power of the government. Burr challenged Hamilton to a duel. Hamilton accepted the challenge. Hamilton was shot by Burr on July 11, 1804. He died the next day.

Alexander Hamilton had a grand vision of the United States of America. Many contemporary historians believe that the United States of America is the nation that Alexander Hamilton envisioned in his federalist policies more than two hundred years ago. Hamilton's vision helped build a strong federal government, which survives today.

Today, we live in a Hamiltonian America.

12

THOMAS KNOWLTON – THE FIRST ARMY RANGER

Thomas Knowlton was born in West Boxford, Massachusetts on November 22, 1740. When Knowlton was young boy, his family moved to Connecticut. The year was 1748. The Knowltons had bought a large tract of land to farm. As a boy, young Knowlton loved to hunt and fish. He spent many hours in the forest near his home honing his skill as a marksman.

Thomas Knowlton fought for the Connecticut militia during the French and Indian War of 1756-1763. So, when the American Revolution started in 1775, Knowlton was already a war veteran. When the fighting began in Massachusetts on April 19, 1775, Knowlton took up arms knowing this fight would be different: this would be a fight for new nation.

As soon as Knowlton heard of the battles at Lexington and Concord, he traveled north to the American camp at Cambridge, Massachusetts. At Cambridge, Knowlton was elected captain in the Ashford Company Fifth Regiment, in the Connecticut militia. Knowlton had returned to the colony of his birth to fight for American liberties. Only two months later, Knowlton distinguished himself as an able leader of men at the legendary Battle of Bunker Hill. Knowlton was second in command of the Connecticut troops under the leadership of General Israel Putnam.

On the night of June 16, 1775, Captain Knowlton received orders to build a redoubt on Bunker Hill. Knowlton's twelve hundred men instead constructed the redoubt on nearby Breeds Hill. Breeds Hill was the smaller of the two hills in Charlestown. It was steeper than Bunker Hill and closer to where the British would land from the Charles River. The men from Connecticut, aided by many other colonial militiamen, worked throughout the night digging and building the little American fort. When the patriots finished the redoubt, they waited for the impending British attack.

Thomas Knowlton

He organized America's first Special Forces unit named, "Knowlton's Rangers".

Early in the morning of June 17, 1775, a British sailor on the H.M.S. Lively spotted the American fortifications. The Lively was moored in the Charles River between Boston and Charlestown. The captain of the Lively ordered the first shots of the grand battle.

Several hours passed. The British were now landing troops on Morton's Point. It was a very hot day. By mid-day, the British started to fire their cannons upon the redoubt. Colonel Prescott of Massachusetts realized that the Americans would be outflanked to the rear of the redoubt, so Prescott ordered Knowlton and his men to fortify an existing rail fence. This fence ran for two hundred yards to the left of the small fort. This hasty maneuver enabled the Americans to stop the first British assault upon the redoubt. Knowlton and his men again held the rail fence throughout a second British charge. It was only when the Americans ran out of gunpow-

der and bullets on the third and final British charge that they had to retreat from the redoubt. Captain Knowlton and his men displayed precise military tactics while covering the retreat of the patriots who were leaving the redoubt.

Knowlton was promoted to major in January of 1776. Knowlton again saw action in Charlestown. Six months later, during the siege of Boston, the new Commander-in-Chief of the American Army, General George Washington of Virginia, sent Knowlton to the occupied town. Knowlton's orders were to raid and burn the enemy quarters. Knowlton was very successful. He lost no men in the small skirmish, and he successfully captured five prisoners and destroyed all the British barracks.

General Washington had recommended that Knowlton be promoted, so on August 1, 1776, Congress made Knowlton a lieutenant colonel. By the end of August, Knowlton was in battle again. This time

Knowlton was fighting at Long Island, New York.

Shortly after the Battle of Long Island, Lt. Colonel Knowlton formed a regiment of elite fighters. They were known as Knowlton's Rangers. They functioned as an advance scouting party. Because of American intelligence failures at the Battle of Long Island, General Washington was now convinced that he needed an elite detachment dedicated only to reconnaissance. General Washington wanted this unit to report directly to him. General Washington chose Knowlton to lead this unit. Knowlton had served in a similar unit during the French and Indian War. He was to lead 130 men and twenty officers. All of Knowlton's men were hand-picked volunteers. They performed a variety of secret missions, most of them too dangerous for regular troops to conduct.

On the morning of September 16, 1776, Knowlton's Rangers fell into a small battle with the British Black Watch

12 THOMAS KNOWLTON

regiment, which was an equally elite fighting force. During this skirmish, the brave hero of the Battle of Bunker Hill was mortally wounded. As he was carried off the battlefield, he was reported to have said to his son, "My son, I am mortally wounded; you cannot do me any good; go now and fight for your country."

Lt. Colonel Knowlton's death was a big loss to the American army. He died an American Revolutionary War hero. After Knowlton died, the Commander-in-Chief praised him by saying, "Knowlton would have been an honor to any country of the world, having died yesterday while gloriously fighting for his beloved country".

Today, the United States Army Intelligence Service has the date of 1776 on its seal. This date is in honor of the inception of Thomas Knowlton's Rangers.

MOSES STOCKWELL – LITTLE BROTHER SEES THREE SURRENDERS

Moses Stockwell was born in Sutton, Massachusetts in 1746. He was the younger brother of Sergeant Daniel Stockwell Jr. Although Moses was two years younger than his brother Daniel, he attained the rank of major in the Continental Army.

Moses met Commander-in-Chief General George Washington on the common green at Harvard University. The year was 1775. All of Moses' male relatives were present at the American camp in Cambridge. Throughout the siege of Boston, in 1775 and early 1776, Moses served the patriot cause with his brother, Daniel Jr., and younger brother, Jonas. His father, Daniel Sr., and several cousins were also at the camp. They were all serving in the Massachusetts militia.

When the British surrendered and evacuated Boston on March 17, 1776, Lt. Moses Stockwell witnessed this joyful event. The enemy had finally been driven out of the town and colony of Massachusetts. After the British evacuation, Moses stayed in Massachusetts for close to fifteen months. During this time, he bought land from his father. It was May of 1777. Moses' new property in Royalston would be the land he would eventually retire upon.[1]

By the summer of 1777, Moses was ordered to Fort Stanwix in northern New York. Moses marched the few hundred miles to Fort Stanwix with his regiment. This new regiment of enlisted men and officers were now in the Continental Army. At Fort Stanwix, Moses was under the command of Colonel Peter Gansevoort.

Meanwhile, a British expedition was making its way south from Canada to New York. The British Army was commanded by

Moses Stockwell

He witnessed three British surrenders in Boston, Saratoga and Yorktown.

General "Gentleman" Johnny Burgoyne. Burgoyne was one of the British generals forced to evacuate Boston, one and one-half years earlier. Burgoyne's plans were to capture and hold all of the Hudson River Valley, all the way to New York City. This action, if successful, would effectively cut off all of New England from the rest of the nation. This plan would hopefully stop the American rebellion.

One of General Burgoyne's objectives was to capture Fort Stanwix. Burgoyne had dispatched over two thousand men under the command of Lt. Colonel Barry St. Legar. In St. Legar's army there was a mixed group of British regulars, Canadians, American torries, Hessian jagers, and American Indians. On his march to Fort Stanwix, St. Legar was informed that the fort had easy defenses to overrun and that it was held by only a handful of Americans. The Americans were badly out numbered. However, there were 750 American soldiers protecting the fort. When St. Legar confidently arrived at the fort, he immediately laid siege to the garrison. Communication had passed from St. Legar to Colonel Gansevoort that the garrison would be spared annihilation if the Americans surrendered. The Americans refused to surrender. They preferred an honorable fight to the death. The presence of St. Legar's Indian allies had convinced the Americans they would not be given any quarter. They knew that they would be massacred if they surrendered.

Colonel Gansevoort requested and received a three-day truce from the British. This ploy enabled Colonel

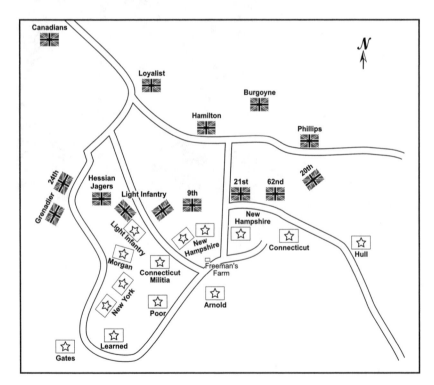

First Battle of Saratoga – Freeman's Farm
Saratoga, New York – September 19, 1777.

MOSES STOCKWELL

Gansevoort to send his second in command, Lt. Colonel Marinus Willet, and newly promoted Major Moses Stockwell on a daring mission that passed through the enemy lines. The two officers were ordered to reach Fort Dayton, some fifty miles away. The Americans were seeking the relief of reinforcements from General Benedict Arnold, General Philip Schuyler, and General Ebenezer Learned. It was August 9, 1777. Lt. Colonel Willet and Major Stockwell left the fort at ten o'clock that night, each armed with nothing but a spear, and provided only with a small supply of crackers and cheese, a small canteen of spirits, and in all other respects unencumbered, even by a blanket. They traveled the whole ensuing day and on the approach of night they dared not strike a light, but lay down to sleep interlocked in each other's arms. Pursuing their journey on the 12th, their little stock of provisions being exhausted, they fed upon rasp-

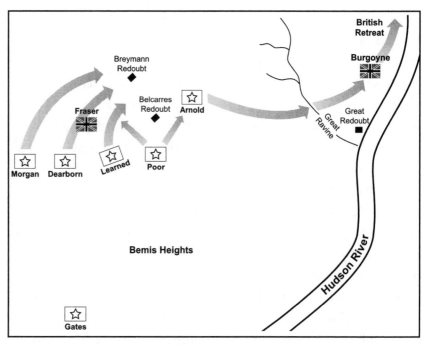

*Second Battle of Saratoga – Bemis Heights
Saratoga, New York – October 7, 1777.*

berries and blackberries, of which they found abundance in an opening occasioned by a windfall. Thus refreshed, they pushed forward with renewed vigor, and at an accelerated pace arrived at Fort Dayton at three o'clock in the afternoon. Willet and Stockwell received a hearty welcome from Colonel Weston whose regiment was then in charge of Fort Dayton and from whom he obtained the agreeable intelligence that

General Schuyler had ordered Generals Arnold and Learned, with the Massachusetts brigade, to march to the relief of Colonel Gansevoort at Fort Stanwix. Then, as a ruse, General Arnold dispatched a half-wit loyalist, called Hon Yost, with false information to give to the British. Hon Yost was to report directly to British Commander St. Legar with tall tales of the exaggerated strength of American reinforce-

13 MOSES STOCKWELL

ments coming to the aid of Fort Stanwix. Hon Yost was a condemned man for plotting to kill American officer, Lt. Colonel John Brooks. Meanwhile, Arnold was keeping Hon Yost's brother as a hostage to ensure that he would complete the mission. Hon Yost did complete the mission with enthusiasm, and the British camp literally started to break up in a panicky departure. Most of the Indians started deserting and turning on their former allies. The Indians even massacred some of the British and plundered anything that they could carry off.

Major Moses Stockwell then took part in the main Battles of Saratoga in September and October 1777. Stockwell, again, was a witness to the surrender of a large British Army on October 17, 1777 at Saratoga. This very important and stunning American victory convinced the French to become militarily involved with the United States against their ancient enemy.

Major Moses Stockwell rejoined General George Washington at the horrible winter camp of 1777-1778 at Valley Forge.[2] Stockwell continued his valuable service to his country and to the Commander-in-Chief throughout the rest of the Revolutionary War. Stockwell saw action at the last battle at Yorktown, Virginia in October, 1781.[3] For a third time, Stockwell witnessed a British surrender. The Yorktown surrender was the final capitulation for the British in the American Revolutionary War.

Shortly thereafter, Major Moses Stockwell returned to Royalston, Massachusetts. After seven long years, Stockwell went home as an American Revolutionary War hero. Waiting for him was his wife Sarah and nine children. Moses and Sarah would later have a family of fifteen children. All of the Stockwell children would one day hear stories of how their father participated in and saw three British surrenders in the War of American Independence.

JOHN GLOVER – FISHERMAN GENERAL

Major General John Glover was born in Salem, Massachusetts in 1732. He was known as a hard-working young man. Glover's family had moved to Marblehead, Massachusetts after his father's death. Through hard work and dedication to his values, Glover eventually became a wealthy fisherman.

Major General John Glover served in the British colonial militia during the French and Indian War of 1756-1763. By 1773, Glover was a captain in the Massachusetts militia. In 1775, he joined the Marblehead Committee of Correspondence. In May 1775, Glover was elected a lieutenant colonel in the Massachusetts militia and took command of the twenty first Massachusetts regiment.

With the onset of the Revolutionary War, Glover helped gather the enlistments of one thousand men. He was then ordered in June 1775 to Cambridge, where Glover first met the new American Commander-in-Chief, General

George Washington of Virginia. Glover was soon promoted to a full colonel. During the siege of Boston, General Washington had ordered Glover to equip and man warships for the protection of all the northern Massachusetts sea ports. Because of this order, Glover is credited with sailing America's first warship. Her name was the "Hannah." In addition, Glover and his courageous men are also considered America's first Marines.

After the siege of Boston ended on March 19, 1776, Colonel Glover and his newly formed fourteenth Continental regiment marched to New York. After the Battle of Long Island,

John Glover
Ferried the American Army across the Delaware River on Christmas night prior to the Battle of Trenton.

★ 14 ★ JOHN GLOVER

Glover and his Marbleheaders exercised a remarkable feat. They evacuated the entire trapped American Army on August 29 and August 30, 1776. They rescued them by boat. The American Army was in a hurried retreat. In a very foggy night, with the British fleet nearby, Glover and his Marbleheaders ferried close to ten thousand American troops, scores of cannon, many horses, and equipment to the safety of New York. All through that night, the sailor-marines rowed their boats back and forth. General George Washington was the last man to get on the last boat. General Washington did this directly under the nose of the British Army. Lt. Benjamin Tallmadge was aboard one of the last boats. He was a witness to this daring epic event. Tallmadge duly noted this event in his memoirs. He watched Glover evacuate the Commander-in-Chief to Long Island after every other patriot soldier was safe. General Washington and

Colonel Glover had assured the nation that the American Army would fight another day.

At Pell's Point overlooking Eastchester Bay, Colonel Glover, along with three other regiments from Massachusetts, formed the brigade that enabled the Commander-in-Chief to withdraw his position at Harlem Heights. Glover's small but important delaying action denied British General Howe from catching and destroying the American Army. Also, at the Battle of White Plains, Glover is said to have given a "good account of himself."

Colonel John Glover is best remembered for the famous crossing of the Delaware River on Christmas evening 1776. During extremely harsh winter conditions, (led by the Commander-in-Chief General George Washington) Glover and his blue-jacketed, white-pants Marbleheaders put across the Delaware River 2,400 troops, eighteen cannon, many horses, and equipment. The American Army then marched

almost ten miles to Trenton, New Jersey, where the Hessian mercenaries were camped. The Hessians were attacked and soundly defeated by the Americans. This American victory was a large morale-boosting episode in the early part of the war. Glover and his Marbleheaders then transported the Hessian prisoners and their captured supplies back across the river.

Within a few months of this dramatic event, Colonel Glover's regiment was disbanded. Most of Glover's men had finished their enlistment time. They went home to support their families. Glover also went home. By summertime, however, Glover returned as a brigadier general, after some coaxing from General Washington.

General Glover was serving with General Gates, when British General "Gentleman" Johnny Burgoyne surrendered his army at Saratoga on October 17, 1777. Glover was ordered to escort the defeated

✦ 14 ✦ JOHN GLOVER

British to Boston. The British boarded ships and sailed to Britain, never to return.

General Glover continued his leadership at Newport, Rhode Island. In 1778, Glover was under the overall command of Major General Lafayette. He commanded a veteran brigade supporting General Sullivan's Franco-American attack in Rhode Island. Glover then succeeded General Sullivan in 1779. Glover rejoined the main American Army under General Washington's command shortly thereafter.

After the British surrender of Yorktown in October 1781, General Glover returned to Massachusetts. The next year he devoted much of his time to recruiting enlistees. Shortly afterward, Glover retired due to ill health. Glover was promoted to a major general in the fall of 1783.

After the war, Major General John Glover continued to work as a successful businessman in Marblehead. He served two terms in the Massachusetts legislature and six terms on the Marblehead Board of Selectmen. He died in 1797, at age sixty four, an American Revolutionary War hero.

TENCH TILGHMAN – FAITHFUL ASSISTANT

The American Revolutionary War of Independence was also a civil war. It was a war that pitted brother against brother and father against son. American patriot Tench Tilghman of Maryland knew this version of war personally, as his father and younger brother were both British loyalists. However, Tilghman continued communications with his father during the war. Neither Tilghman nor his father held any animosity toward the other for his political views. This was unusual during this troubled period of time. Many families were torn apart and actually participated in killing each other. Tilghman's loyalist family members were noncombatants and continued to live in the United States during and after the war. Tilghman also knew what it was like to put a successful business on hold, as he liquidated his merchant business in 1775. He then became the secretary and treasurer of the Continental Congress that same year.

It was at the Continental Congress that Tilghman met George Washington. Tilghman became a captain in the Pennsylvania militia, and shortly after the Declaration of Independence, Tilghman became the military secretary and aide-de-camp to General George Washington.

Captain Tilghman saw his first military action with General Washington at the disastrous Battle of Long Island, on August 27, 1776. The Battle of Long Island was a poor performance on behalf of all the Continental generals. The British command was simply masterful with General Howe making all the correct strategic moves to trap the Americans. Howe inflicted heavy

Tench Tilghman
General Washington's faithful assistant served without pay for two years. He informed Congress of the American victory at Yorktown.

✦ 15 ✦ TENCH TILGHMAN

losses on the American Army. General Howe's only mistake was to let the Americans evacuate when he didn't pursue a total victory. Almost three weeks later, the American Army was engaged with British forces at the Battle of Harlem Heights on September 16, 1776. While the Americans did not gain a military victory, they did give a much better account of themselves. The Americans stood "toe to toe" with the British regulars. Both armies actually retreated during the battle, first the Americans, then the British. When the fleeing British pulled back, General Washington ordered his men to stop the pursuit. Captain Tilghman said, "The pursuit of the fleeing British Army was so new a scene that it was with difficulty that our soldiers could be brought upon to retire and stop the chase. The men gave out a loud "hurra" and left the fighting field in good order."

Captain Tench Tilghman continued his service as the personal secretary to the Commander-in-Chief, at the victorious Battle of Trenton, New Jersey, on December 26, 1776, and at the Battle of Princeton, New Jersey, on January 3, 1777.

In April 1777, Tilghman was given the rank of lt. colonel by the Continental Congress. Technically, Tilghman had been serving as a volunteer secretary to General Washington until the Commander-in-Chief petitioned the Congress and insisted that he receive his commission. General Washington said, "Captain Tench Tilghman has been a zealous servant and slave to his nation and a faithful assistant to me for years. He has during this time refused to receive pay. His honor and gratitude interest me in his favor and I wish for him to obtain his commission."[1] This letter from General Washington contained the praise and honor that Tilghman earned and deserved while serving his nation.

To follow the career of Lt. Colonel Tench Tilghman during the revolution would be to write the history of the American Army. In the letter already quoted, it is stated that Lt. Colonel Tilghman was in every action in which the main American Army participated. Tilghman suffered in the debacle of the Battle of White Plains. With pain, he witnessed the fall of Forts Lee and Washington. He followed in the humiliation and retreat of the dissolving army through the "Jerseys" into Pennsylvania and crossed the Delaware River on Christmas night during a severe storm. He reveled in the victory at Trenton. Lt. Colonel Tench Tilghman saw the defeat at Brandywine and the action at Germantown, and shared in the terrible sufferings at Valley Forge. Lt. Colonel Tilghman moved south with the Commander-in-Chief when the war moved into the southern states. Finally, he was at Yorktown, Virginia, participating in the operations of the memorable siege and surrender, which effectively ended British rule in America. Beside the Commander-in-Chief was Lt. Colonel Tench Tilghman, who, having gone through the whole war, was now a witness to its ending. Tilghman's journal of the siege and surrender of Yorktown is one of the few first hand records of the battle and British surrender. Tilghman wrote the following: "In the morning, Lord Cornwallis put out a letter requesting that twenty four hours might be granted to commissioners to settle terms of capitulation for the surrender of the posts known as York and Gloster. General Washington answered that two hours only would be allowed to send out terms in writing. Cornwallis accordingly sent them out, generally as follows: that the men in the Garrisons should be made prisoners of war, the Germans and British soldiers to be sent to England and Germany. General Washington answered that the terms of sending troops to England and Germany were inadmissible. Cornwallis closed

with all the terms, except those of acceding to the same honors, as those granted at Charleston, South Carolina. The commissioners who met for us were Lt. Colonels Laurens and Viscount Norailles–on the part of the British, Colonel Dundas and Major Ross."[2]

Immediately upon the signing of the articles of surrender, General Washington selected Lt. Colonel Tench Tilghman to ride to Philadelphia to inform the Congress of the British capitulation. Tilghman arrived in Philadelphia four days after the surrender on October 24, 1781, in the middle of the night. The news spread quickly and soon all the patriots of Philadelphia were rejoicing in the news of the stunning victory. Tilghman presented a letter to Thomas McKean, President of the Congress of the United States, of the joyous news from Virginia. Within this dispatch, General Washington was quick to remember his trusted secretary

and aide-de-camp when he said, "Sir, Colonel Tilghman, one of my aides-de-camp, will have the honor to deliver the joyous news to you. He will inform you of every instance which is not mentioned in my letter. His merits, which are too well known to all, have gained my particular attention, and I hope they may be honored by the notice of your Excellency and Congress."[3]

On the following day, October 25, 1781, a committee of Congress passed a series of resolutions expressing the nation's thanks to General Washington and General Lafayette, and to all the officers, soldiers, and sailors of the United States and France. Lt. Colonel Tench Tilghman was honored with the presentation of a horse and a sword by the Board of War.

After the war, in the summer of 1783, Lt. Colonel Tench Tilghman married his cousin, a common occurrence in the eighteenth century. He was discharged from the army on

★15★ TENCH TILGHMAN

December 23, 1783. Tilghman then entered into a business partnership in Baltimore with one of the financiers of the revolution, Robert Morris. Tilghman died only three years later in 1786.

General Washington knew the importance of having such a trusted secretary and aide-de-camp as Lt. Colonel Tench Tilghman. General Washington depended upon his young officer and grew to respect and love him during their common ordeal to free the nation. General Washington grew quite despondent upon learning of Tilghman's death. General Washington wrote to the Tilghman family and said, "Amidst all the sorrowing that are mingled on this melancholy occasion, I may venture to assert that excepting those of his nearest relatives, none could have felt his death with more regret than I did, because no one entertained a higher opinion of his worth or had imbibed sentiments of greater friendship for him than I had done. Amidst all your grief, there is this consolation to be drawn; that while living no man could be more esteemed, and since departed, none more lamented than Lt. Colonel Tilghman."[4]

BENJAMIN LINCOLN – LOCAL POLITICIAN

Benjamin Lincoln
Lincoln accepted the British surrender at Yorktown on behalf of the Continental Army.

Benjamin Lincoln was a successful farmer when the colony of Massachusetts Bay revolted against British rule in April of 1775. Born in 1733, Lincoln was also a military man and a local politician. He was a lt. colonel in the Massachusetts militia. He had also served for two decades as a local politician from the community of Hingham. Lincoln served as a representative in the Massachusetts colonial legislature and the Provincial Congress. He was a well-respected man in Massachusetts, and an important member of the Committee of Correspondence. The Committee of Correspondence was just another name for the Committee of Safety or the Sons of Liberty. This secret society was comprised of patriot radicals. They were the men who led the rebellion against British rule in the thirteen colonies. Lincoln was one of these men.

Benjamin Lincoln, as did most of his peers, felt American independence was worthy of a fight. One of Lincoln's reasons for pursuing independence was that the "common man" could not own property in Europe. Why did this fact trouble him so much about a continent far across the ocean? Lincoln felt that European royalty held too much power over their people. Free men could own property in the colonies, but Lincoln was concerned that these rights might be taken away by the British Crown. Lincoln was waging war so that these rights would never be taken away in the new land of opportunity. For Lincoln, this land was Massachusetts and the other twelve colonies of America.

In 1775, Lincoln was under the direct command of General George Washington. This was during the siege of Boston. In 1776, Lincoln was promoted to major general in the Massachusetts militia. He helped train the American troops camped in

✦ 16 ✦ BENJAMIN LINCOLN

Cambridge. Lincoln rejoined the Commander-in-Chief in New York later that year. He had stayed behind in Boston, with orders to clear Boston harbor of British vessels after the evacuation of the city.

The Commander-in-Chief General George Washington, knowing that Lincoln held only a Massachusetts militia commission, wrote to Congress asking for a Continental Army commission. General Washington got his wish. Lincoln and sixteen other men were appointed major generals. In his letter to Congress, General Washington said, "Lincoln is an excellent officer worthy of command in the Continental Line."

Major General Lincoln participated in the Battle of White Plains, New York. Three months later, in January 1777, Lincoln and his 6,000 troops from Massachusetts were fighting alongside General William Heath of Massachusetts in the disastrous attack on Fort Independence. At this battle, the Americans, emboldened by the recent victories at Trenton and Princeton, believed that they could drive the enemy forces out of New Jersey. Initial victories along the route toward Fort Independence encouraged the Americans to demand a surrender of Fort Independence. The Hessian commander ignored the American demand to surrender. Instead, he started to fire his cannons at the American Army. The Americans, instead of attacking Fort Independence, started to fall back. They were making plans to attack the fort at a later time. The indecisiveness of the American command allowed the enemy to regroup and attack American positions near the fort and inflict heavy losses on the American Army.

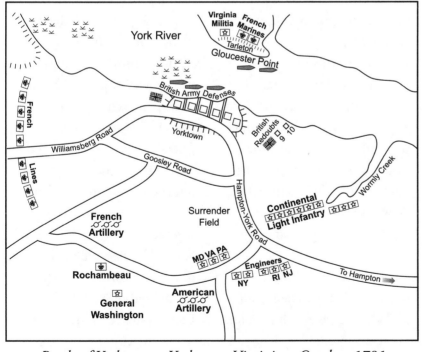

Battle of Yorktown – Yorktown, Virginia – October, 1781

BENJAMIN LINCOLN

By early 1777, Lincoln rejoined General Washington at Morristown, New Jersey. It was here that Lincoln received his Continental Army major general commission. Lincoln was ordered to Delaware, but was reordered shortly afterwards to join General Schuyler in northern New York. The Americans were trying to stem the progress of British General Johnny Burgoyne's offensive coming down from Canada. Upon arriving at the American camp to take command of the New England militia, Major General Lincoln successfully quelled a potential disaster. He discovered that General John Stark of New Hampshire, then in charge of the New England militia, refused to recognize the authority of Congress. Stark felt that he had been overlooked in the promotion as a major general. Stark was still serving as only a militia general, and told Lincoln that he only took orders from the people who gave him his commission. He would not

take orders from a Congress who had ignored him. Major General Lincoln, needing Stark and his men, allowed Stark to continue in his command and let him participate in the Battle of Saratoga, regardless of his insubordination. Luckily for the American cause, excellent results were produced. General Burgoyne surrendered his army to the Americans and this development opened up the involvement of French military participation on behalf of the American patriots.

During the Battle of Saratoga, Major General Lincoln unfortunately received a severe leg wound that would put him out of action for nearly a year. Lincoln went home to Massachusetts, where he was rehabilitated, but the injury left him permanently lame.

On his return to active duty, Lincoln marched from Philadelphia to South Carolina. He was appointed by Congress to command the Southern American Army. He enjoyed

some early successes in small skirmishes, but on May 12, 1780, he surrendered Charleston, South Carolina to the British. A large British Army commanded by General Henry Clinton surrounded the city of Charleston. The Americans were badly out numbered, nearly six to one. The Americans, after a gallant fight, ran out of provisions. The Americans were reduced to loading their guns with scrap iron and glass. With the capitulation of the city, Lincoln was made a prisoner of war. He was, however, paroled by the enemy in exchange for British officers. He returned to Philadelphia waiting for orders.

Major General Lincoln returned home to Massachusetts to raise recruits and supplies for the Continental Army. He then took command of troops near the British stronghold of New York City. Lincoln marched his troops to rejoin the Commander-in-Chief General George Washington in the siege of

16 · BENJAMIN LINCOLN

Yorktown, Virginia in 1781. When British General Lord Cornwallis capitulated, Lincoln was the American general who officially accepted the British sword at the surrender ceremonies. During the surrender, the British band played a song called, "The World Turned Upside Down." American and French victors looked on with pride at their stunning victory.

After Yorktown, Major General Lincoln accepted the position of Secretary of War. He held this position from 1781 to 1784. He was also a member of the convention in 1788 that ratified the United States Constitution. He became Lt. Governor of Massachusetts in 1788. Lincoln published extensive papers describing the climate and soil of Maine, entitled, "Observations on the Climate, Soil and Value of the Eastern Counties in the District of Maine," he also published a paper on the state of native peoples, entitled "Indian Tribes, the Causes of their Decrease, Their Claims, etc." Lincoln died at his home in Hingham, Massachusetts in 1810 at the age of seventy seven. This local politician had served his nation well. He was an American Revolutionary War hero.

17

SALEM POOR – RECOGNIZED COURAGE

At least three dozen African-Americans are known to have fought with the twelve hundred patriots at the legendary Battle of Bunker Hill on June 17, 1775. But the General Court of the Massachusetts Bay Colony recognized the courage of only one soldier during that battle: a patriot named Salem Poor. Unfortunately, not much is known about Salem Poor. We do know that he was born into slavery in Andover, Massachusetts, in the late 1740s. The General Court issued a proclamation in honor of Salem Poor in December 1775, only six months after the battle. The document said, "Salem Poor behaved like an experienced officer, and in this man centers a brave and gallant soldier." Fourteen officers signed the document, including the Massachusetts commanding officer, Colonel William Prescott. Prescott had fought alongside Poor in the small earthen redoubt.

During the night of June 16, 1775, Salem Poor's regiment, under the command of Colonel William Prescott, was sent to Bunker Hill to build fortifications in Charlestown. At the battle, Poor is said to have slain the popular British officer, Major John Pitcairn, as well as many other British "redcoats" during the fierce battle. Pitcairn led the third and final fatal charge of British marines on the American redoubt. Pitcairn was the same British officer who, only two months earlier, marched the regulars to Lexington and Concord in a failed attempt to capture Sam Adams and John Hancock.

In 1776, Salem Poor and the newly formed Continental Army marched to New York. Poor saw action again at the Battle of Saratoga. This important American victory convinced the French to become militarily involved on behalf of the Americans. Poor also endured the hardships of the cold winter camp at Valley Forge in 1777-1778.

Salem Poor

He was the only soldier recognized by the Massachusetts Bay Colony for valor at the Battle of Bunker Hill.

17 SALEM POOR

The professionalism and bravery of Salem Poor and other African-American soldiers unfortunately did not persuade the Continental Congress to enlist more African-American patriots. Southern representatives to the Continental Congress opposed this measure. Their states feared that if many African-Americans enlisted, slaves would revolt and fight for the British. The Northern delegates, anxious for unity, joined with the Southern delegates. The Continental Congress ordered General Washington to stop recruiting African-Americans.

By 1777-1778, the war was going badly for the American Army. General Washington's manpower crisis continued to grow. By early 1778, General Washington was desperate for American soldiers. General Washington decided to defy Congress. General Washington continued to enlist African-Americans. Congress had little choice but to approve General Washington's decision. The American states subsequently began to offer freedom to slaves in return for their military service.

Salem Poor was an American fighting for the liberties that he was denied at birth. There is no record of his death. His courage at the Battle of Bunker Hill made him an American Revolutionary War hero, and his patriotism will forever stand as an example to all Americans who cherish freedom.

ABIGAIL ADAMS – REMEMBER THE LADIES

Abigail Adams stood on a hilltop near her farm in Braintree, Massachusetts. It was June 17, 1775. Abigail Adams, along with her seven-year-old son John Quincy, watched the epic Battle of Bunker Hill unfold several miles away on the Charlestown peninsula.

That evening she wrote a letter to her husband John Adams. John was in Philadelphia, Pennsylvania, serving as a representative from Massachusetts in the First Continental Congress. She wrote to lament the facts of the day to John. It would be one of the many letters she would write to him during the revolution. She wrote that the Americans had inflicted heavy casualties on the British and that she feared total warfare was now imminent. Her words were prophetic; the war had already begun.

Abigail Adams had no formal schooling. However, she eagerly gathered knowledge from her extensive reading of literature and history. She always spoke her mind and gave her opinion on public issues to John and the other revolutionary leaders.

Abigail Adams had learned to cope with her absent politician husband. For many years, John Adams had been serving as a diplomat both at home and abroad. Abigail Adams subsequently became a successful merchant and farmer. Self-taught and self-reliant, she learned how to farm and manage a business. She was a prominent woman of her era. When John returned home, he would consult with her on the pressing issues of the day. He often referred to his wife as "my top advisor." Probably John didn't always agree with Abigail, but he knew she had many valid and heartfelt suggestions. Unlike most women of her day, Abigail Adams supported women's rights. John, however, was reluctant to support women's rights. He thought the new nation was not ready for women's rights. Abigail Adams pushed for better education for females. One of her famous

Abigail Adams
She fought for women's rights and advised her husband John.

★ 18 ★ ABIGAIL ADAMS

suggestions to her husband was, "Remember the Ladies." She was one of America's first abolitionists. She spoke out against slavery. She understood that the institution of slavery was contrary to everything that the United States stood for.

In the summer of 1784, after the United States secured independence from Britain, Abigail Adams rejoined John Adams in France. He was on a diplomatic mission and had just recently signed the Treaty of Paris.

Abigail Adams continued to advise her husband. Although not an official diplomat of the United States, she promoted the new American nation to her French friends. Abigail Adams became good friends with Martha Washington when John Adams was serving as Vice-President. John was in the first and second administrations of President George Washington. In 1796, after Washington's term ended, John Adams was elected as the second president of the United States. When John Quincy

Adams became the sixth president of the United States, in 1824, Abigail Adams became the first woman to be both wife and mother to a president of the United States.

Abigail Adams rests with her husband John Adams in the United First Parish Church in Quincy, Massachusetts. She died in Massachusetts in 1818 of typhoid fever, at age seventy three.

19

PHILLIS WHEATLEY – POETIC INSPIRATION

In 1753, a girl was born in Senegal, on the west coast of Africa. When she was seven, African slave traders kidnapped her and sold her to British slave merchants. That terrible event brought her to Boston, in the new and strange land called America. The wealthy Wheatley family of Boston bought her. Slaves were bought and sold in both the north and south in America during the eighteenth century. Fortunately, the Wheatleys treated the black girl as one of their own children and renamed her Phillis. Her African name has been lost to history. Susannah Wheatley educated her and brought her up.

By the age of thirteen, Phillis Wheatley could read and write not only English, but Greek and Latin as well. Her strong character enabled her to overcome the early childhood trauma of being kidnapped and she soon had some of her poems published because of her talent. Phillis Wheatley became the first important African-American poet.

Phillis Wheatley was freed from slavery by the Wheatley family at age twenty, in 1773. Shortly thereafter, she was invited by abolitionists to travel to England. There she became a symbol for freedom and a celebrity among the anti-slavery movement in London. Because of her travels to Britain, Phillis Wheatley was able to become friends and later corresponded with eminent people in England, such as the Countess of Huntingdon, the Earl of Dartmouth, and Reverend George Whitefield.

Phillis Wheatley continued to write her poems before and during the Revolutionary War. Months before the British evacuated Boston in March 1776, she wrote a poem exalting American Commander-in-Chief General George Washington. In her poem to General Washington entitled, "To His Excellency George Washington," she writes

Phillis Wheatley

First African-American poet of notoriety. She fought for the abolition of slavery.

⋆ 19 ⋆ PHILLIS WHEATLEY

these stanzas: "Anon Britannia droops the pensive head, While round increase the rising hills of dead, Ah! Cruel blindness to Columbia's state! Lament thy thirst of boundless power late. Proceed, great chief, with virtue on thy side, Thy ev'ry action let the goddess guide. A crown, a mansion, and a throne that shine. With gold unfading Washington! Be thine." General Washington read the poem and was so impressed he invited her to meet him personally at his headquarters. General Washington wrote, "I thank you most sincerely for your polite and elegant lines. However, undeserving I am of your gracious tribute, your style and manner exhibit a striking proof of your poetical talents. If you should ever come to Cambridge, or near head-quarters, I shall be happy to see a person so favored as yourself." Phillis Wheatley accepted the invitation and traveled to Cambridge only a few days before the British evacuated Boston. General Washington's staff

received her graciously and respectfully. She talked with the Commander-in-Chief for at least half an hour.

Phillis Wheatley continued to write. She fell in love with a wealthy African-American, John Peters. Her life with John Peters and her children was fine until 1784, when John Peters fell into debt. Tragically, this setback sent the family into poverty. Two of their older children died, and shortly thereafter, Phillis Wheatley and her youngest child both fell sick and died in the same bed, only hours apart in 1784. This was a tragic end to a very talented woman who inspired many abolitionists in the United States.

The abolitionists of nineteenth century America continued to read and remember Phillis Wheatly. The abolitionists reprinted her poems and writings before and during the American Civil War of 1861-1865. Phillis Wheatley had a clear vision of freedom for all African-Americans. For

many years Phillis Wheatley inspired those wishing to abolish slavery. She warned America when she wrote, "Thus the splendors of the morning light, The owl in sadness seeks the eaves of night. No more, America, in mournful strain, Of wrongs and grievance unredressed complain; No longer thou shall dread the iron chain, Which wanton Tyranny, with lawless hand, Had made, and with it meant t' enslave the land."

Today, Phillis Wheatley remains a role model and is a true American heroine.

19 PHILLIS WHEATLEY

An Hymn to the Morning

Attend my lays, ye ever hon-
our'd nine,
Assist my labours, and my
strains refine,
In smoothest numbers pour
the notes along,
For bright Aurora now
demands my song,
Aurora hail, and all the thousand dies,
Which deck thy progress
through the vaulted skies:
The morn awakes, and wide
extends her rays,
On ev'ry leaf the gentle
zephyr plays;
Harmonious lays the feath-
er'd race resume,
Dart the bright eye, and
shake the painted plume,
Ye shady groves, your ver-
dant gloom display,
To shield your poet from the
burning day:
Calliope awake the sacred
lyre,
While thy fair sisters fan the
pleasing fire:
The bow'rs, the gales, the
variegated skies,
In all their pleasures in my
bosom rise,
See in the east th'illustrious
king of day!
His rising radiance drives the
shades away—
But Oh! I feel his fervid
beams too strong,
And scarce begun, concludes
th'abortive song.

        – By Phillis Wheatley

20

PAUL REVERE – THE REGULARS ARE OUT

"The regulars are coming; the regulars are out," shouted the horseback rider galloping at full speed. The man on the back of John Larkin's horse was a patriot rider for the Sons of Liberty named Paul Revere. The date was April 18, 1775. Revere was on his famous ride. It ended on April 19, in the early morning. Revere reached Lexington and Concord, ten miles east of Boston, with the news of British soldiers, also known as regulars, marching out of Boston. Along the way, Revere warned many local minutemen of Middlesex County to be ready for a battle.

Earlier in the evening of April 18, Revere had seen the signal of the two lanterns. They were hanging in the bell tower of the North Church. The sexton, Robert Newman, had placed them there. Revere knew he had to act to warn the patriot countryside of the British march. The Sons of Liberty knew that one lamp meant the British would come by land; two meant they would come by sea. This was the warning of the British exit from Boston. Both Revere and Billy Dawes saw the two lanterns signaling the water-bound exit of the British. Revere crossed the Charles River by boat to meet John Larkin in Charlestown. Dawes rode out from Boston Neck, a small strip of land connecting Boston to the mainland. Both men were quick to spread the alarm of the hostile British advance. The British had two aims. First, they wanted to confiscate the gunpowder being stored in Concord by the Massachusetts militia. Second, they wanted to capture the two leading patriots of Massachusetts, Samuel Adams and John Hancock.

By British decree, Hancock and Adams were the only members of the radical Sons of Liberty who would not be given clemency. They were the most wanted men in the colony of Massachusetts

Paul Revere

This Son of Liberty became famous for his midnight ride. He was the leader of the mechanics in Boston and was an accomplished silversmith.

and probably would have been sentenced to death if captured and tried in court. Revere managed to find and warn the two leading patriots of their intended capture. He then continued on to warn the countryside.

Many years before April 19, 1775, Revere was already a leading citizen of Boston. He was a leader of the mechanics. A mechanic in the eighteenth century was a man who worked in a trade. Revere was a very clever man and an active patriot. He held the title of grand master in the Masonic brotherhood of Massachusetts. Because of this position, he had gained influence with many people. Revere's career and political views brought him into the circle of professional men such as Dr. Joseph Warren, Hancock, John Adams, Sam Adams, James Otis, and the traitor Dr. Benjamin Church, who was later revealed to be a British spy and banished from the colony. Revere would ride correspondence for

the Committee of Safety to New York City and Philadelphia and to other members of the inter-colonial Committee of Safety.

Revere was one of the organizers of the famous Boston Tea Party. Revere, along with the professional revolutionary, Samuel Adams, organized a group of Masons to destroy the British tea trade in New England. On December 16, 1773, Revere and several dozen rebels disguised themselves as Mohawk Indians. They boarded British merchant ships anchored in Boston Harbor. In protest of the British tea tax, they threw overboard 342 chests of tea valued at $90,000, a large fortune in the eighteenth century.

Revere was also a master engraver. He memorialized the victims of the Boston Massacre in a well-known engraving of the bloody scene. Revere printed the first issue of American Continental Currency. He made the first official seal for the State of

Massachusetts. This seal is on the state flag of Massachusetts today. When it was time for the ratification of the United States Constitution, Revere worked very hard for its implementation.

By 1778-1779, Revere was a lt. colonel. He was in command of Castle William in Massachusetts Bay. He was given a field command shortly thereafter and was ordered to be ready to attack the enemy at the Penobscot River in the Massachusetts territory of north-central Maine.

At the end of the Revolutionary War, Revere continued his trade as a silversmith. He is credited with developing significant metallurgy and founding practices. He also worked in portrait engraving, songbooks, political cartoons, coats of arms, and manufactured dental devices. Revere also cast bells and cannons. Revere's foundry made spikes, bolts, and copper accessories for the famous U.S.S. Constitution, the vessel affectionately known as "Old

★ 20 ★ PAUL REVERE

Ironsides." Today, the U.S.S. Constitution is the oldest active American Naval warship. It is stationed at the Charlestown Naval Yard in Boston.

Paul Revere had sixteen children by two wives. His first wife, Sarah Orne, died on May 3, 1773, and after a short interval he married Rachel Walker on September 23, 1773. Each wife bore him eight children. Revere died on May 10, 1818, at age eighty three.

Paul Revere wore many hats for his new nation. He was here, there, and seemingly everywhere at once. Revere will always remain the American Revolutionary War hero who rode out on a cold April night warning the countryside, "The Regulars are coming; the Regulars are out!"

Paul Revere and Billy Dawes' Ride

Let me tell you about the night in '75,
It's all about Paul Revere and Billy Dawe's ride,
Off they went with two strong steeds,
The regulars are out, so patriots take heed,
With quick, strong steps and scarlet coats,
Then across the Charles went Paul in his boat,
One by land and two by sea,
His majesty's boys in Lexington by three?
And off went Billy through the Back Bay,
The lesser known of the two heroes today,
The Charlestown road, Paul did take,
Through Medford and Metotomy for
Adams' sake,
Dawes arrived first to warn the town,
The Regulars are coming, they are bound,
Along the road Paul met some foes,
Got captured awhile, so there he laid low,
But the hero broke free and off he fled,
I must make it to Hancock is what he said,
So early in the morning, Paul arrived,
To tell Adams and Hancock that they must hide,
Then the patriot men gathered on the green,
Standing tall to greet the British scene,
So off rode the duo in the middle of the night,
To help launch a nation's maiden flight,
So for ever and ever, they'll ride again,
The all night ride of America's men.
— *By Marc Stockwell-Moniz*

21

HAYM SOLOMON – PRIME NEGOTIATOR

In every successful enterprise, men and women such as American patriot hero Haym Solomon work tirelessly in the background. Haym Solomon was a European Jew who immigrated to America from Poland in 1772. Solomon then became a successful merchant in New York.

Solomon spoke French fluently as well as several other languages. He was a prime negotiator for the United States during the Revolutionary War. Solomon secured loans and subsidies from France and Holland that financed America's war efforts. He also personally gifted to the United States $600,000, an enormous amount of money in the eighteenth century.

In 1778, the British accused Haym Solomon of spying. Solomon was put in prison, but managed to escape. He fled to Philadelphia and continued to work in his brokerage and commission business. He became an assistant to Robert Morris, Superintendent of the Office of Finance in Philadelphia in 1781.

Haym Solomon helped design the United States dollar bill. The Jewish Star of David is on the back of the dollar bill just above the American eagle. General George Washington, who was a Christian and a Mason, insisted that the Star of David be displayed on the dollar bill to honor the Jews who helped the patriot cause in the American War of Independence.

In 1782, Haym Solomon was also a major contributor to the first synagogue built in Philadelphia, the Congregation Mikveh Israel. The nation's first Hebrew school was instituted by the Congregation Mikveh Israel.

Haym Solomon was a patriot who fought and worked very hard for the political and religious rights of all Americans. Of course, Solomon was not the only Jewish person who fought in the American Revolution. Other Jews served as soldiers and sailors.

Haym Solomon

Worked with Robert Morris to finance the Continental Army. He negotiated loans from European nations on behalf of the United States.

HAYM SOLOMON

Phillip Russell was a surgeon at Valley Forge; Colonel Davis Franks was an aide-de-camp to General Washington. A "Jew Company" fought in South Carolina during the Southern campaign. Moses Myers fought in Virginia, and the Sheftall family fought and lost everything when they were captured in Savannah, Georgia. Twenty two Jewish patriot soldiers are buried at Manhattan's Chatham Cemetery. Many Jews sacrificed their lives for their new country. There is new evidence that a Jewish soldier, Abraham Solomon, participated in the Battle of Bunker Hill. He was a member of Colonel John Glover's 21st regiment from Gloucester.

Haym Solomon understood the uniqueness of the United States of America. He worked tirelessly to help secure and preserve the freedoms we enjoy today. Haym Solomon died in 1785 an American Revolutionary War hero.

SAMUEL ADAMS – PROFESSIONAL REVOLUTIONARY

Samuel Adams failed miserably in business. But he was one of the most successful and radical revolutionaries in America. Born in Boston on September 22, 1722, Samuel Adams became a professional revolutionary. He was at his best when he was harassing the British military occupiers of Boston.

Samuel Adams's revolutionary career started in 1764 when he started to oppose British rule. With direct verbal attacks on British colonial governor Hutchinson, Adams soon became a menace to British authorities. Two years later in 1766, Adams led the more radical elements of the Massachusetts patriot movement in gaining control of the Massachusetts House of Representatives. Adams helped organize the successful opposition to the Townshend Acts of 1767. The Townshend Acts were new revenue-implementing systems for the customs commissioners. The Townshend Acts taxed paper, paint, glass, and tea imported into the colonies to pay for military

expenses and the salaries of royal officers. The colonial assemblies, however, argued that they alone held the power to tax the people and not the British Crown. When the Townshend Acts were repealed, except for the tax on tea, some colonists were satisfied to remain under British rule. Adams however, kept up the organization to British opposition in the early 1770s.

Samuel Adams was a leading force in the formation of the Sons of Liberty, a secret society formed to oppose the Stamp Act and other repressive British measures. In the early 1770s, Adams was exporting his firebrand, revolutionary politics to the sister colonies. He helped organize the famous Boston Tea Party of 1773. Adams led the opposition to the Intolerable Acts (also known as the Coercive Acts), a British attempt to punish Bostonians for the Boston

Sam Adams
Leader of the patriot movement in Boston. He signed the Declaration of Independence.

★ 22 ★ SAMUEL ADAMS

Tea Party. This measure prohibited the loading or unloading of merchant ships in the port of Boston until all the monetary damages of the Boston Tea Party were recovered. Adams, naturally, strongly supported the Suffolk Resolves, which declared the Intolerable Acts illegal. Dr. Joseph Warren – later the martyr of the Battle of Bunker Hill – had drafted the Suffolk Resolves, which also urged the people of Massachusetts to withhold any form of tax to the British crown and to form their own government.

By 1775, the leading patriot-politicians of all the American colonies were finally speaking the language of radical Samuel Adams and demanding complete independence from the mother country. The British military governor of Massachusetts, General Gage, declared martial law. He issued an arrest warrant for Adams, along with his political cohort, John Hancock. Gage proclaimed that all rebels in arms and their abettors would be offered a pardon, if they would return to the allegiance of the British crown – all except Samuel Adams and John Hancock. These two men were the only Boston patriots not offered immunity from prosecution.

One reason the British decided to march to Lexington and Concord on the night of April 18, 1775 was to find and capture these two patriot leaders. Adams and Hancock were hiding at Reverend Jonas Clark's house. Eight minutemen guarded Clark's house. Paul Revere arrived at the house in the early morning. He warned Adams and Hancock of the approaching British march. On the fateful day of April 19, 1775, the British did not find either Adams or Hancock, but instead found that the American Revolutionary War had begun. When the "shot heard around the world" was fired that morning, Adams' dream had been achieved.

Samuel Adams was a member of the First and Second Continental Congresses in Philadelphia. He was a signer of the Declaration of Independence. Adams drafted the world's oldest English language constitution, the Constitution of the State of Massachusetts. It is still the state constitution today. Adams served as the lt. governor of Massachusetts from 1789 to 1793. Upon the death of Governor John Hancock in 1793, Adams became governor and held the office until 1797.

When Samuel Adams died in 1803, he did not leave this world a wealthy man. However, this Revolutionary War hero left the new nation of the United States rich in freedom and liberty that he fought long and hard to establish.

DR. JOSEPH WARREN – BUNKER HILL MARTYR

A medical doctor and major general, a martyr for liberty's cause, and an American hero who died at the Battle of Bunker Hill: his name is Joseph Warren.

Dr. Warren was born in 1741, to an old Massachusetts Bay family from Roxbury. In 1759, Warren was graduated from Harvard Medical School in Cambridge. Several years prior to the American Revolution, Warren had become acquainted with the revolutionary leaders of Massachusetts. These patriot leaders were his patients.

Dr. Warren became interested in politics. He started to work with Samuel Adams. Warren drafted the Suffolk Resolves, which proclaimed the Intolerable Acts to be illegal. He argued that the people of Massachusetts should withhold any and all taxes to the British crown. Warren also encouraged the people to form their own government. Warren was a member of the Committee of Safety along with Adams, John Hancock, James Otis, and Paul Revere. Warren was a gifted writer and orator and gave many speeches demanding the removal of the British military occupation of Boston. On the anniversary of the Boston Massacre, Dr. Warren gave a stirring speech reminding the local patriots of the British atrocities.

On the eventful evening of April 18, 1775, Dr. Warren dispatched both Paul Revere and Billy Dawes on their midnight rides to Lexington and Concord. They rode to warn the countryside about the British regulars marching out from Boston. The British mission was to confiscate the patriot gunpowder stored in Concord and capture both Hancock and Adams. The next day, April 19, 1775, the American Revolution began. Shots were fired at Lexington and Concord. Warren was called out to the alarm, along with many other Massachusetts patriots. Warren took an active part in the day long battle, which chased the British back to Boston.

On April 23, 1775, Dr.

Dr. Joseph Warren

First American patriot leader to die for his nation. He fought gallantly at the Battle of Bunker Hill.

✦ 23 ✦ DR. JOSEPH WARREN

Warren succeeded Hancock as the President of the Massachusetts Provincial Congress. He quickly organized the militia army of Massachusetts and was elected a major general.

On June 15 and June 16, 1775, the Americans made plans to fortify the high ground of Bunker Hill, on the Charlestown peninsula. Warren was with the Provincial Congress in Watertown. On the legendary battle day of June 17, 1775, Warren left the safety of the Provincial Congress. He was informed of the British soldiers' landing in Charlestown. Warren then hastened to join the New England minutemen at the redoubt on Breeds Hill. The Americans had fortified Breeds Hill, not Bunker Hill as was planned. Although smaller than Bunker Hill, Breeds Hill was steeper than Bunker Hill and therefore easier for the Americans to defend. The redoubt on Breeds Hill was commanded by Colonel William Prescott of Massachusetts. Warren was

reported to have been sick that day. He was suffering from exhaustion. Regardless, he mounted a horse and sped to Breeds Hill. When Warren arrived to the delight and the cheering of the patriots, Prescott immediately offered his command to him. Warren refused to take command. He said he came only as a volunteer. His commission as a major general had yet to arrive at the American camp. Warren wanted to serve where he would be most useful and that was with the ranks of his men in the redoubt. During the third and final British charge up Breeds Hill, and the subsequent orderly retreat of the Americans, Warren stood alone before the ranks. He attempted to rally and encourage the men by his example. He fought valiantly while the Americans in the redoubt were being hotly pursued by the enemy. Warren was killed instantly when an English officer who knew him borrowed a musket from one of his soldiers and fired a bullet

into his head.[1] Warren had set aside his status as a revolutionary leader to be with his men, and was where he felt he was needed the most on the day he became a martyr for his new undeclared nation.

The British buried Warren in a mass communal grave on Breeds Hill. His body was later dug up by the Americans and was identified because of the two artificial teeth that Paul Revere had made for him. Warren was then buried with full military honors.

Major General Dr. Joseph Warren was a heroic revolutionary leader of Massachusetts and the martyr of the Battle of Bunker Hill. Warren was the first revolutionary leader to fight and die for his country. Warren was thirty three years old when he died. A grand memorial is dedicated to his memory. It now stands next to the Bunker Hill Monument at the hallowed ground battle site in Charlestown, Massachusetts.

WILLIAM PRESCOTT – THE WHITES OF THEIR EYES

On April 18, 1775, William Prescott was at his farm in Pepperall, Massachusetts. The next evening, Prescott was receiving military orders at the American camp in Cambridge, Massachusetts. The American Revolutionary War had begun.

When hostilities erupted on April 19, 1775, William Prescott was a farmer. He was a forty-nine-year-old military veteran, having fought in the French and Indian War of 1756-1763. Although Prescott missed the military action of April 19, 1775, he was present and accounted for at the "council of war." The men at this "council of war" were the leading military men of Massachusetts. The other officers present at the council were Generals Ward, Heath, and Whitcombe; Colonels Bridge, Frye, James Prescott, Bullard, and Barrett; and Lt. Colonels Spaulding, Nixon, Whitney, Mansfield, and Wheelock. William Prescott and his fellow Massachusetts officers were now leading the nation into unknown territory.

Colonel Prescott is best remembered as one of the American commanders at the Battle of Bunker Hill. He oversaw the Massachusetts troops. Most of the Massachusetts men at the battle were in the small earthen redoubt, on top of Breeds Hill. Prescott's steadfast leadership on June 17, 1775 held the militia together on that ominous day.

Before the battle began, the British fired a cannon ball. The British considered the American resistance to be sheer folly, and they intended the cannon ball to be a warning only. Unfortunately, the cannon ball decapitated Asa Pollard of Billerica. The soldiers

William Prescott

Commanded troops at Bunker Hill. He is credited with saying, "Don't fire until you see the whites of their eyes."

✦ 24 ✦ WILLIAM PRESCOTT

requested that Pollard be buried with the customary religious services, but Prescott deliberately denied the request. Prescott wanted his men to concentrate on their duties and prepare for the imminent bloody battle. Prescott felt that if his men had any time to ponder the fate of this fallen soldier, or had time to ponder their own fate, they wouldn't be as effective as they could be.

Colonel Prescott is often given credit for the famous words "Don't fire until you see the whites of their eyes." Whether it was Prescott or General Israel Putnam who gave the famous orders, or possibly both of them, the men in Prescott's command strictly obeyed these orders. Gallantly, the American patriots performed as professional soldiers during the battle and throughout their orderly retreat.

Before the epic battle began, Prescott had been roaming on top of the redoubt. It was a very hot day. At the same time, General Gage of the

British Army was looking at Prescott through his field glasses from across the Charles River in Boston. Gage didn't know who Prescott was. Gage turned to his aide, Abijah Willard, and asked him if he could identify the American commander. Willard looked through the glasses and in astonishment told Gage that it was William Prescott. It was Willard's own brother-in-law! Gage asked Willard if Prescott would fight. Willard replied, "Yes sir, he is an experienced soldier. He will fight you as long as there is one ounce of blood in his veins. I cannot answer for his men, General, but Prescott will fight you to the gates of hell." This was the reputation that Prescott carried. At this moment, General Howe realized that the grand British Army would be in for a long, bloody fight to capture the high ground of Breeds Hill. Gage ordered the redoubt to be taken immediately.

As the British were about to launch their mid-day attack,

Major General Dr. Joseph Warren arrived from the American headquarters at Watertown. Warren said that he had come to fight as a volunteer. Prescott offered Warren command of the redoubt. However, Warren refused. Warren praised Prescott when he told him, "I will enjoy learning from a soldier of your experience and I wish to fight where I am needed the most."

The British climbed steep Breeds Hill and attacked the American redoubt two times. Twice the "redcoats" were repelled by the shattering fire of the patriot muskets. On the third and final charge up Breeds Hill, the British succeeded in gaining entry to the little earthen fort. The Americans had finally run out of gunpowder and bullets. Hand-to-hand combat ensued. During the American retreat, Dr. Joseph Warren was shot in the head and died instantly. Prescott, ordered his men to continue the retreat. Meanwhile, Thomas Knowlton's men were stationed at the rail fence and supported the retreat from the redoubt. Almost all of the patriots made it out of the redoubt to the safety of the American camp in Cambridge.

The British had managed to "gain the day". However, the British would feel the consequences of the Battle of Bunker Hill throughout the next eight years of fighting. Bunker Hill was the first momentous battle in the American War of Independence. The British victory had been shallow, disastrous, and humiliating. The British had often ridiculed the Americans, yet their best troops, led by their best officers, had been repeatedly repulsed by Prescott's men. The fledgling American Army gained confidence at the Battle

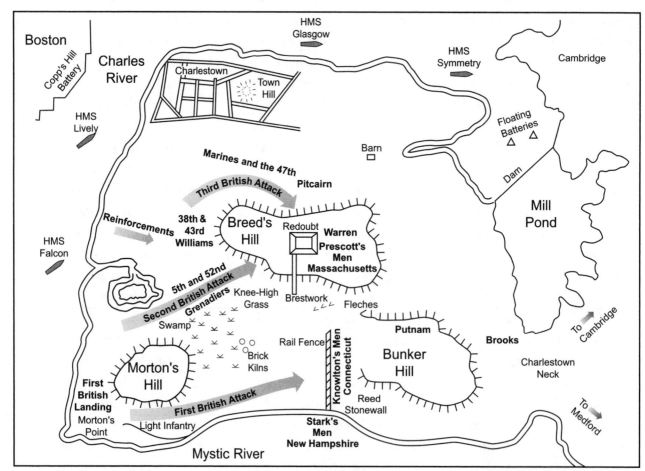

Battle of Bunker Hill – Charlestown, Massachusetts – June 17, 1775.

✦ 24 ✦ WILLIAM PRESCOTT

of Bunker Hill. They proved to themselves and to the British that they could stand up to the best army in the world.

Samuel Adams wrote to American diplomat, Elbridge Gerry, "Until I visited our camp in Cambridge, I never heard of the valor of Prescott at Bunker Hill." The honorable American statesman Daniel Webster said, "If there was any commander-in-chief at Bunker Hill, it was Prescott. From the start of the ground breaking, to the retreat, Prescott acted the most important part; and if it were proper to rename the battle, from any distinguished soldier in it, it should be called Prescott's Battle."

Colonel William Prescott fought in the American War of Independence for two more years, at Long Island, New York. He also took part in the action at Kip's Bay. Prescott helped defeat British General "Gentleman" Johnny Burgoyne at the Battle of Saratoga. Shortly afterward, Prescott retired to his home in 1777, due to an old farm related injury.

Colonel William Prescott of Massachusetts was an inspiring and well-respected leader. He was exactly the type of leader the American nation required in the moment of its greatest need. Prescott is memorialized with a large bronze statue at the foot of the Bunker Hill Monument.

Colonel William Prescott is an American Revolutionary War hero. He helped free his nation of tyranny. He died at home, at age sixty nine, on October 13, 1795.

JOHN PETER MUHLENBERG – THE FIGHTING PREACHER

Imagine yourself sitting in your house of worship. You are listening to the sermon. Your congregational leader, while preaching to the faithful, removes his religious garments and reveals the full regimental dress uniform of a Virginian colonel. That is exactly what John Peter Muhlenberg did at the end of one Sunday sermon in 1776. Nobody knew that Lutheran clergyman Muhlenberg was preaching his final sermon. Nobody knew he was going to war. But Muhlenberg, paraphrasing Ecclesiastes 3:1, said, "There is a time for all things. There is a time to preach and a time to pray; but there is also a time to fight and defend our nation, and that time has now arrived."

In January, of 1776, and at the invitation of General George Washington, Muhlenberg accepted the rank of colonel in the Virginia militia. He had decided the best way to recruit troops was to be first in line, so he set a dramatic example. He had great success that Sunday. Many men followed his lead. Muhlenberg was able to enlist almost three hundred of his congregation to fight for American liberties.

In March 1776, Muhlenberg was given command of Virginia's eighth regiment. His men became known as the German Regiment. They immediately marched south to assist in the defense of Charleston, South Carolina. Muhlenberg and his German Regiment also successfully defended Fort Sullivan against British General Clinton's expedition in the Battle of Sullivan's Island.

Before tensions arose between Britain and her American colonies, Preacher Muhlenberg had already been an important figure in the local politics of Virginia, having served as chairman of the Committee of Public Safety in Dunmore County. In

John Peter Muhlenberg

Lutheran preacher commanded Virginia's eight regiment.

1774, he was elected to the Virginia House of Burgesses. During this time, Muhlenberg first met General George Washington.

In February 1777, Muhlenberg was commissioned a brigadier general. At Brandywine, on September 11, 1777, Muhlenberg's brigade stopped the enemy from advancing through a narrow valley. Retreating Americans were able to reform their regiments, behind the protection of the Virginians. Muhlenberg is given credit for stopping the British attack. His actions allowed the American Army to escape and fight another day. Less than a month later at Germantown, Muhlenberg led his men deep into enemy territory and was able to fight his way back, despite a large British manpower advantage. With the Commander-in-Chief, Muhlenberg and his men spent the horrendous winter of 1777-1778 at Valley Forge.

In the summer of 1778, the Virginians fought at the Battle of Monmouth. Muhlenberg and his men entered the battle rather late. However, they did not have much impact on the outcome. The Battle of Monmouth ended in a draw. The Continental Army fought well, inflicting over 350 British casualties, but the Americans suffered an equal amount of losses.

Later in 1778, the Virginians were assigned to General Israel Putnam's division. Putnam was camped near the Hudson River in New York. In July 1779, Muhlenberg's men saw action at Stony Point. He was fighting alongside General Anthony Wayne. Muhlenberg and his men helped capture the strategic position at Stony Point. In December 1779, General Washington sent Muhlenberg to take command in Virginia, where Muhlenberg continued to influence young men to join the patriot cause.

During the Yorktown campaign, General Muhlenberg commanded the brigade that assaulted British redoubt Number 10. Muhlenberg, along with Colonel Alexander Hamilton, captured the redoubt. This action helped secure valuable ground for the final American assault.

Promoted to major general on September 30, 1783, John Peter Muhlenberg retired and moved to Pennsylvania, where he lived among Pennsylvania Germans and was regarded as a national hero, second only to General George Washington. In 1784, Muhlenberg was elected to the Supreme Executive Council of Pennsylvania. From 1785 to 1788, Muhlenberg was the Vice President of the state of Pennsylvania, under President Benjamin Franklin. Muhlenberg served in Congress as a representative from Pennsylvania. In 1801, he was elected a United Sates Senator from Pennsylvania. President Thomas Jefferson appointed him Supervisor of the Revenue of Pennsylvania and he later became Collector of Customs in

★ 25 ★ JOHN PETER MUHLENBERG

Philadelphia, for the remainder of his life. He died in 1807.

John Peter Muhlenberg was a clergyman and a major general. He was an ardent American patriot. He was also an American Revolutionary War hero. Muhlenberg defended his actions in the war when he told his brother, "I am a clergyman, it is true, but I am a member of society as well as the poorest layman, and my liberty is as dear to me as to any man. Shall I then sit still and enjoy myself at home when the best blood of the continent is spilling? I am called by my country to its defense. I obey without hesitation! And so far, am I from thinking that I am wrong? I am convinced it is my duty to do so, a duty I owe to my God and to my country."

FRANCIS MARION – THE SWAMP FOX

Swamp Fox, Swamp Fox where are you going to be? How can the British ever capture thee? Swamp Fox, Swamp Fox riding high and low; you are here, you are there, you are everywhere we know.

Born in 1732, General Francis Marion was a militia officer from South Carolina. Marion participated in many battles and skirmishes in the Southern campaigns of the American Revolutionary War. In 1775, as a delegate to the South Carolina Provincial Congress, Marion was named a captain in the second South Carolina regiment. Shortly thereafter, Marion participated in driving out the British Royal Governor from the colony.

Promoted to major in February 1776, the Swamp Fox commanded the left side of Fort Sullivan. He successfully defended the fort in June 1776. Marion personally armed the cannons that prevented British ships from entering Charleston Harbor. He was promoted to lt. colonel of that year and soon took leave to nurse a bro-

ken ankle. During this time, the British captured Charleston in May 1780. However, the Swamp Fox's activities as a superb guerrilla fighter had just begun.

With his four dozen horseback-riding fighters, Marion quickly reeled off successive patriot victories at Blue Savannah, Black Mingo, and Tearcoat Swamp. Marion soon gained the attention of the British Commander-in-Chief, Lord Cornwallis. Cornwallis dispatched one of his more brutal officers to fight Marion. His name was Major Banastre Tarleton.

Tarleton was the leader of the British Light Dragoons. Tarleton and his men were fast-moving, horseback-riding soldiers. Tarleton often trailed the Swamp Fox for days but never caught him. Sometimes, Tarleton was within a few miles of Marion. Tarleton felt secure that he would eventually capture Marion. At the same moment that Tarleton felt he was

Francis Marion
Guerrilla leader was known as the "Swamp Fox".

★ 26 ★ FRANCIS MARION

about to catch his prey, Marion would be watching the British from some dark nook of a morass. At nightfall, Marion would strike Tarleton's flank with a keen and severe attack. The Swamp Fox continued to harass British and loyalist forces and their supply lines throughout the war. Marion's mode of operation would be to vanish into the swamps of South Carolina to his hiding base of Snow's Island. From Snow's Island, Marion sent out his men in every direction. Almost daily, Marion had a confrontation with the enemy.

In December 1780, the Swamp Fox was promoted to brigadier general by patriot Governor Rutledge. Marion organized what would be known as Marion's Brigade. Marion's Brigade became the terror of British and Tory outposts. Marion continued his guerrilla operations and occasionally cooperated with General Green and the Continental Army. British Commander Cornwallis was determined to wipe out the Swamp Fox, but his efforts to destroy him were fruitless. The only damage the British could ever muster upon the Swamp Fox was the destruction of his camp at Snow's Island.

With the American victory at Yorktown, Virginia in 1781, American independence was all but assured. Marion was appointed commandant of Fort Johnson and was elected to the state senate of South Carolina in 1782, and re-elected in 1784. Marion retired from the military in 1783, at his rank of brigadier general. He emerged as a legendary American Revolutionary War hero. Marion participated in South Carolina's Constitutional Convention in 1790. He died in 1795.

William Cullen Bryant wrote a song about the Swamp Fox called, "Song of Marion's Men." It started with these lines; "Our band is few, but brave and tried. Our leader intrepid and bold; the British soldier trembles, when Marion's name is told."

Brigadier General Francis Marion was the Swamp Fox.

27

JOHN HANCOCK – "THE KING WILL NOT NEED SPECTACLES"

Orphaned as a young boy, John Hancock was adopted by a wealthy paternal uncle. Hancock graduated from Harvard University in 1754. Ten years later, in 1764, Hancock inherited his uncle's business and soon became the richest man in Boston.

With his growing wealth and business dealings, Hancock became friends with many wealthy loyalists. Hancock, however, had different political views than his Tory friends. The rebels of Massachusetts, with their idea of liberty, had won Hancock's mind. By the early 1770s, Hancock's new friends included the professional-revolutionary-firebrand Samuel Adams, the orator of liberty James Otis, the writer of the Suffolk Resolves, Dr. Joseph Warren, and the Sons of Liberty messenger, the mechanic Paul Revere. Hancock had become a revolutionary.

On every anniversary of the Boston Massacre, Hancock would give stirring speeches to the Boston populace.

Many early American fortunes were amassed by wholesale smuggling. The affluent and haughty John Hancock was known as the "King of Smugglers." Hancock smuggled tea into Boston on merchant ships, and lost money whenever British tea made its way into the teacups of New Englanders. So, in 1773 Hancock helped organize the Boston Tea Party.

In October 1774, the Provincial Congress of Massachusetts appointed a Committee of Safety, and made Hancock the leader of this committee. In this powerful position, Hancock could call out the colonial militia and provide ammunition and provisions to them. The Provincial Congress at this time disavowed any attempts to attack the British Army. Nevertheless, their ultimate goal was to drive the British out of Boston, and they took measures to stop supplies from reaching the British.

John Hancock

First signer of the Declaration of Independence. He was a leader of the Sons of Liberty in Boston.

★ 27 ★ JOHN HANCOCK

By early 1775, the British realized that Hancock and Adams posed a genuine threat. Hancock and Adams became the most wanted men in America. If caught, both men would have been sentenced to death as traitors to the British Crown. They were the only patriot leaders to whom the British wouldn't give clemency.

On the night of April 18, 1775, Hancock and Adams knew the British would soon attempt to arrest them. They were hiding out together in Lexington. The British troops, led by Lt. Colonel Smith and Major John Pitcairn, intended to capture them, and also to secure the patriot gunpowder in Concord. But that evening, Dr. Joseph Warren sent Paul Revere and Billy Dawes out from Boston to warn Hancock and Adams about the British march to Lexington. Revere found both Hancock and Adams early in the morning of April 19, 1775, and warned them of the advancing British soldiers. Hancock and Adams managed to flee from Lexington and escaped to the safety of Woburn. Meanwhile, Revere continued his ride toward Concord and warned the countryside of the marching British.

The British reached Lexington by five o'clock in the morning. They found Massachusetts militia leader Captain John Parker with fewer than seventy armed men on the Lexington green. The Americans were making a military stand. Major Pitcairn ordered the Americans to put down their arms. Some of the Americans were disarming when a single shot was fired. Several other shots quickly followed. When the shooting was over, eight Americans lay dead, with only one British soldier wounded. The "shot heard around the world" had been fired. The British continued on to Concord and fought a day-long battle all the way back to Boston. The British took many casualties on their return to Boston. The American Revolution had begun.

On May 19, 1775, Hancock was elected President of the Continental Congress. He was replacing Peyton Randolph, who had just died. Hancock believed that he should and would be named Commander-in-Chief of the fledgling American Army. The army, after all, was composed mainly of soldiers from Massachusetts. But the Continental Congress bypassed Hancock in favor of a Virginian with military experience. The Virginian was Colonel George Washington. This decision upset the wealthy patriot from Massachusetts, but Hancock accepted the decision with tact because he knew it was in the best interests of the fledgling nation.

Little more than a year later, on July 4, 1776, Continental Congress President John Hancock was the first American to officially rebel against British King George III. Hancock was the first patriot to sign his name on the Declaration of Independence.

✦ 27 ✦ JOHN HANCOCK

Hancock signed his name in a large bold hand, so King George would not have to put on his spectacles to read it.

John Hancock did have a military role during the revolution. In 1778, he was appointed a major general in the state militia of Massachusetts. He commanded six-thousand men in defense of Newport, Rhode Island. On September 1, 1780, Hancock became the first American governor of Massachusetts. He served all but two years, because of illness, from 1780 until his death in 1793. In 1785, Hancock was again elected as the President of the United States Congress. However, he was unable to serve due to ill health. In 1778, Hancock was elected President of the Massachusetts State Convention that ratified the United States Constitution. Massachusetts was the sixth state to ratify the Federal Constitution under Hancock's guidance.

John Hancock risked everything, including his own life, for the sake of the new nation. He became one of the leading rebels of the American Revolution. Hancock had great confidence in his new nation. Many Americans had faith in his leadership. Hancock was also generous. He helped support many needy families in Massachusetts during the hard times of the American Revolution. He died in Massachusetts in 1793 at the age of fifty-six.

JAMES OTIS – SOWING SEEDS OF THE REVOLUTION

Sam Adams gained fame as the "heart and soul" of the American Revolutionary movement. James Otis, however, was the embryonic seed who inspired all the revolutionaries in America, including Sam Adams, Dr. Joseph Warren, John Hancock, John Adams, Patrick Henry, Thomas Paine, and Paul Revere.

In his famous speech given in Boston, Massachusetts on February 24, 1761, Otis argued against the Writs of Assistance. The Writs of Assistance gave colonial customs officers the authority to search warehouses and homes, to exact any "illegal contraband." Otis, a prominent Boston lawyer, argued that any law that was against Natural Law, such as the Writs of Assistance, was in itself void. Natural Law is based on the fact that all individuals are born with and entitled to certain intrinsic rights. These are rights that no government can take away. They are the right of popular sovereignty, the right to revolt, democracy, liberty, and the pursuit of happiness. These powerful ideas were later instituted in the American Declaration of Independence by the Founding Fathers of the United States. When President John Adams commented many years later on the speech that Otis gave, he said, "Otis was a blaze of fire! He burned every British tie before him. Our independence was born, then and there."

Since his famous speech of 1761, James Otis had argued against the royal governor's attempt to gain greater authority. He also questioned the limits of authority by the King and Parliament. He called upon the people to resist the British government, claiming that, although Parliament was a sovereign body, it was not all powerful.

When the Stamp Act was introduced by Parliament in

James Otis

He was a Massachusetts lawyer who inspired the Boston revolutionary movement.

March 1765, Otis was the only delegate from Massachusetts who was not a supporter of the measure. Otis was at the Stamp Act Congress arguing against the measure. The Stamp Act was designed to raise money to pay the cost of maintaining British troops in America. The stamps were affixed on all printed material, including newspapers, broadsides, pamphlets, land grants, and all legal documents. Also, advertisements, calendars, playing cards, liquor licenses, and even dice were affixed with the stamps. The stamps were a way to show that the royal tax had been paid on the item.

If James Otis could prevail and persuade the British Parliament of its folly, the quartering of British troops would not be at the expense of the people of Massachusetts. Otis said, "If an army must be kept in America at the expense of the colonies, the Parliament must allow each colony to assess its quota and raise the monies as easily to themselves as might be, and not to have taxes levied and collected without our consent."

When James Otis was arguing against the British Parliament's omnipotence, he said, "To say Parliament is absolute and all powerful before her subjects is a contradiction. The Parliament cannot make 2 and 2, 5: its perceived omnipotence cannot do it. The supreme power in a state belongs to God. Parliament can declare what is good for the whole of society; however, the declaration itself does not make it so. There must be God as a higher authority. God's natural laws are immutably true and everlasting and any Parliamentary declaration against the will of the people would be contrary to eternal truth, equity, justice, and ultimately void."

James Otis, not surprisingly, was threatened with treason on a few occasions by the British authorities in Boston. His speeches would often inspire violence in some of the more radical elements of Boston society. However, Otis was quick to resist any effort to use armed resistance against the British troops in Massachusetts.

America's first revolutionary suffered a crushing blow, on the evening of September 5, 1769. Otis was in a fit of rage. He confronted British officers in a coffee house in Boston. Otis demanded an apology from them. Some of his letters had been intercepted and rumors were circulating that he was provoking disloyalty. These charges were hardly untrue. Unfortunately, for Otis, his own violence erupted in that Boston coffee house. While fighting one of the British officers, he received a severe blow to the head. This injury drove Otis in and out of madness for the remainder of his life. He was finished as a lawyer and career revolutionary. Otis was eventually declared legally insane in December 1771. Otis did, however, have some lucid moments. He managed to fight for American liberties at the

★ 28 ★ JAMES OTIS

Battle of Bunker Hill on June 17, 1775.

James Otis lived long enough to see his nation throw off the yoke of British subjugation. A revolutionary movement that he had started more than two decades earlier had come to fruition, with an independent United States of America. This new nation was full of the rights and liberties for which Otis had fought so long and hard.

James Otis died in 1783, while watching a summer thunderstorm. He was struck by lightning and killed instantly. Otis is buried at the "Old Granary Cemetery," close to his fellow revolutionaries, Sam Adams, John Hancock, Paul Revere, and Robert Treat Paine, in downtown Boston.

JOSEPH PLUMB MARTIN – YOUNGSTER FOR FREEDOM

When the American Revolutionary War began in 1775, Joseph Plumb Martin was only fourteen years old. Martin was born on November 21, 1760, in Berkshire County, in western Massachusetts. When Martin was seven years old, he went to live with his grandparents in Milford, Connecticut. Unfortunately, Martin had to leave home because his father could not properly support all of his children.

When Martin found out about the fighting at Lexington and Concord, on April 19, 1775, he wanted to enlist in the Connecticut militia. His grandfather, however, would not allow him to leave home and march off to the war. Although Martin's grandfather supported the patriot cause, he told Martin he was too young to fight. Within a year and a half, however, Martin decided to enlist for a six-month period of time without his grandparent's permission. Martin ran away. He enlisted in the Connecticut militia in early July, 1776, only a few days after the Declaration of Independence. With his enlistment, neither Martin nor his grandparents realized that it would be 1783 until he would come home to start his life as a carpenter.

After his enlistment, Martin and the Connecticut militia marched to New York to reinforce General George Washington and the Continental Army. In New York, young Martin participated in a few skirmishes or small battles prior to the big Battle of Long Island. Martin describes his first encounter with wounded men when he said, "We now began to meet wounded men after the battle, another sight I was unacquainted with, some with broken arms and legs, and some with broken heads. The sight of these a little daunted me, and this made me think of home, but these sights

Joseph Plumb Martin

Martin's Revolutionary War Military Records. He fought for seven years under General Washington.

★ 29 ★ JOSEPH PLUMB MARTIN

and thoughts quickly disappeared."

Joseph Plumb Martin quickly became a seasoned veteran. And he was only fifteen years old! Many of the hardships that would befall Martin and the American Army started at the campaign for New York City. At Kip's Bay and Harlem Heights, on September 15 and 16, 1776, Martin recalled that the encounters with the British were "sharp skirmishes." These skirmishes helped to elevate American morale despite enduring hardships. The Americans fought well against the powerful British. Martin said, "We stayed on the battlefield till nearly sunset, expecting the enemy to attack us again, but they showed no interest. The men were tired and faint, having had nothing to eat in forty eight hours and I amongst the rest." Martin continued, "We remained here till sometime in the month of October without anything happening excepting starvation and that had by this time become a sec-

ondary matter. Hard duty and nakedness were considered the foremost evils, as the weather began to cool and we had to be almost every night on the cold and often wet ground without a blanket."

Joseph Plumb Martin received his discharge from the Connecticut militia on Christmas Day, 1776. He immediately left for home. Martin would be at home, however, for only four months. He rejoined the Continental Army in April and returned to fight in New York. He was stationed at the Hudson Highlands, guarding against a possible British invasion from Canada.

The Continental Army then marched to Pennsylvania. There, Martin participated in the Battle of Germantown on October 4, 1777. As the winter was settling in, Martin continued in the defense of his country at the horrible winter camp at Valley Forge, in 1777-1778.

At Valley Forge, Joseph Plumb Martin was assigned to

a "foraging party." Foragers were responsible to gather as many supplies as could be found in the surrounding countryside. Foraging expeditions rounded up any cattle, hogs, turkeys, geese, and other livestock that could be found. Whenever possible, the soldiers bought supplies. Sometimes they stole provisions. They were often destitute, with very little money. When possible, the American soldiers encouraged and cajoled farmers to sell cheaply to the foraging parties. Available supplies, however, could not meet the needs of the American Army. The deprivations of the army continued throughout the long, harsh winter at Valley Forge. Martin said of these conditions, "We were now in a truly forlorn condition, no clothing or food and disillusioned. There was no remedy, or alternative to this plight except dispersion. But dispersion was not thought of. We engaged in the defense of our injured country and we were determined to persevere as

✦ 29 ✦ JOSEPH PLUMB MARTIN

long as the hardships were not altogether intolerable. The hardships of military life, the year before, were nothing in comparison to what I had suffered in this present campaign. We were in danger of perishing in the midst of a plentiful land."

Joseph Plumb Martin and the Continental Army did persevere the winter of 1777-1778. They rebounded and fought again in the spring. The Continental Army emerged from Valley Forge as a professional army having been trained by General Baron von Steuben.

On June 28, 1778, Martin and his fellow Americans fought very well as professional soldiers, at the Battle of Monmouth. Although the battle did not produce a total victory, the Americans held the British Army to a draw. Martin at this time served with the Light Infantry Brigade. The Army's first line of defense depended upon the Light Infantry Brigade to hold the American line. When Martin was not in battle, he was on guard duty and always alert for any British advance party.

Another year passed. It was December 1779. Joseph Plumb Martin settled into winter quarters at Morristown, New Jersey. Martin was still with General George Washington and the Continental Army. Again, the winter weather was very severe. The familiar hardships returned. The resilient American Army knew these hardships all too well. Again they persevered. Martin recalled his time at Morristown saying, "We continued starving and freezing, until sometime in February."

When the campaign of 1780 began, Joseph Plumb Martin became a corporal and joined the Corps of Sappers and Miners. Sappers and Miners were men who dug trenches under enemy positions to undermine enemy fortifications by laying mines to blow them up. They also fortified camps, opened or repaired roads in advance of the army, and were considered a special operations battalion. If a soldier in the Corps of Sappers and Miners became a prisoner of war, he would most likely be executed because of the fear and destruction that this unit of soldiers created.

In 1781, Joseph Plumb Martin, after a brief time on furlough, found that his corps had left New York. They were marching toward Virginia under the command of General Lafayette. Martin proceeded to travel by foot, alone, three hundred miles to catch up with the army. His solo trek took him from Connecticut to Annapolis, Maryland, where he finally arrived at the American camp. Almost immediately, Martin returned with the Corps of Sappers and Miners to West Point, New York to defend the northern border.

With the joyful news of the arrival of the French fleet, General George Washington decided to march his army to Virginia. Commandant de Grass commanded the French fleet. They were sailing north to

★ 29 ★ JOSEPH PLUMB MARTIN

Virginia from the West Indies. The American plan was to trap the British Army in Virginia. With the allied rendezvous completed, and with the entrapment of the British successful, the siege of Yorktown commenced. Joseph Plumb Martin and the Corps of Sappers and Miners dug the front-line trenches. The Continental Army and the French allies used these trenches to "bottle-up" and trap General Lord Cornwallis and the British Army.

On October 19, 1781, after a two-day ceasefire, the British and Hessian troops surrendered to General George Washington and the victorious American Army. Joseph Plumb Martin was a witness to this wonderful event and said, "The British Army marched out, drums beating and they stacked their arms. We marched to the right-hand side of the road, our French allies to the left. The British did not make a good appearance. They felt their honor was wounded while their German allies did not care. The war had ended for them. The British were led out by General Charles O'Hara and was escorted by our General Benjamin Lincoln, who accepted the formal surrender sword."

Joseph Plumb Martin would remain in the army two more years. Peace negotiations dragged on until the Treaty of Paris concluded the war. The hostilities officially ended in October 1783 and Martin was finally discharged.

Joseph Plumb Martin would eventually settle in Prospect, Maine as a carpenter. For the rest of his life, Martin was a well-known Revolutionary War veteran. Martin often relived his youth with stories that he told to the children of Prospect. His stories were about the youngster who fought for freedom. His name was Joseph Plumb Martin.

DANIEL MORGAN – THE OLD WAGONER

Daniel Morgan was a rough and tough frontiersman. He was born in the wilderness of Hunterdon County, New Jersey, in 1736. He was the first cousin of Daniel Boone. Morgan left home at age seventeen, after he had a disagreement with his father. Morgan traveled south to Virginia, where he gained a reputation as a hard-working man who liked to drink and fight.

During the French and Indian War, Morgan was working for the Virginia militia. Under the command of the British military, Morgan was working as a teamster driving a horse-drawn wagon. A teamster was also known as a wagoner. When Morgan first met George Washington, Washington was a lieutenant colonel in the Virginian militia. Both men were fighting against the French. An ugly incident that forever marked Morgan's dislike of the British occurred, when a British officer hit Morgan with the flat side of his sword. This event happened while Morgan was delivering supplies to

the army. Morgan proceeded to hit the officer and knocked him out with one punch from his big hand. He was court-martialed and received five hundred lashes on his bare back as punishment. Years later, Morgan would joke that the British still owed him one more lash because they miscounted the lashes.

With his tough attitude and hard-working ethic, Daniel Morgan was learning how to be a leader of men. In April 1775, hostilities broke out between the British and the Massachusetts colonists at Lexington and Concord. Morgan had been preparing himself for this fight. He knew he could recruit troops. On June 22, 1775, when the news of the epic Battle of Bunker Hill reached Virginia, Morgan was commissioned a captain in the Virginia militia. He led ninety six

Daniel Morgan
He defeated British dragoon leader Banastre Tarleton at the Battle of Cowpens.

DANIEL MORGAN

sharp-shooting riflemen over six hundred miles to Cambridge, Massachusetts. They arrived in late July at the American camp. Upon their arrival, Morgan re-met General George Washington, who was now the Commander-in-Chief of the American Army.

In September of 1775, Captain Daniel Morgan was issued orders to accompany General Benedict Arnold to Canada. In this failed American attempt to conquer the city of Quebec, Canada, an ill equipped American Army fell short of taking the city. Arnold received a severe leg wound. Morgan then assumed command. Although the Americans fought hard and gallantly, the American attempt to make Canada the fourteenth colony had failed. After the battle, Arnold had escaped, but Morgan was captured by the British. Morgan returned to the United States, however, after having been paroled and exchanged for British prisoners of war in the fall of 1776.

By November 1776,

Morgan was promoted to the rank of colonel. He was in command of five hundred sharpshooters. Morgan rejoined General George Washington in Pennsylvania. Morgan and his men participated in the Philadelphia campaign. From Pennsylvania, Morgan was ordered to New York to reinforce General Gates.

Colonel Morgan fought at the Battle of Saratoga and is credited with stopping the British advancement. In October 1777, Morgan's Virginia riflemen inflicted heavy losses on General Johnny Burgoyne's regulars. He was one of the American officers who enjoyed the first big victory by the United States over the British. This victory ultimately led to the military participation of France in the war as an ally of America.

Colonel Morgan and his Virginia riflemen again rejoined General George Washington. The main American Army was at its winter quarters at Valley Forge. It was a brutal, cold

winter camp in 1777-1778. Colonel Morgan and his men suffered all the hardships that befell the American Army at Valley Forge. Starvation and disease were common.

Colonel Morgan resigned his commission in 1779, because he felt insulted, having been passed over for promotion to brigadier general. By 1780, Morgan rejoined the Continental Army. Congress offered Morgan command of the Southern theater of the war. Morgan accepted. His vindication for command was complete.

In 1781, General Daniel Morgan again contributed greatly to the American fight for independence. At the Battle of the Cowpens, Morgan defeated the "British Butcher," Colonel Banastre Tarleton, and his dragoons. Morgan did this with strategically placed riflemen and cavalry charges. At the Cowpens, the American cavalry charges were led by Colonel William Washington, a kinsman of the Commander-in-Chief. British General Lord

★ 30 ★ DANIEL MORGAN

Cornwallis had sent Tarleton to dislodge the Americans with a large force of cavalry and British riflemen. Tarleton hotly pursued Morgan until reaching the Cowpens, about three miles from the North and South Carolina border. It was at the Cowpens that Morgan rallied his troops. In one general charge upon the enemy lines, Morgan's men scattered the British in every direction. Tarleton's squadron of cavalry, seeing the panic of the British regulars, fled for their lives. This battle was disastrous for Cornwallis, as ten commissioned officers and 129 soldiers were killed, with another twenty nine officers and two hundred men wounded, as well as five hundred men becoming prisoners of war. Large quantities of arms and ammunition were also confiscated. Losses to Morgan and the American Army were just twelve killed and sixty wounded.

The American victory at the Cowpens was a prelude to the Yorktown campaign nine months later. General Daniel Morgan, or the "Old Wagoner," as his men fondly called him, displayed magnificent leadership. He achieved a stunning victory over the best troops that Lord Cornwallis could deploy against him. Morgan's tactics, while employing his excellent marksmen, enabled his troops to rout a larger British Army. Morgan thus secured his place in the annals of the American Revolutionary War as a great leader of men.

General Daniel Morgan retired after the Battle of the Cowpens because of a recurring pain in his hip. This pain made it impossible for him to ride a horse. He finished out the war at his home in Virginia.

In 1790, the United States Congress honored Daniel Morgan with a gold medal struck in his honor for his heroic victory at the Cowpens. Morgan became a successful land speculator after the war. In 1797, he was elected to Congress from Virginia for one term. The "Old Wagoner" died on July 2, 1802.

JOHN PAUL JONES – I HAVE NOT YET BEGUN TO FIGHT

In the late eighteenth century, British school children would read about the tales of the famous "pirate" John Paul who terrorized the British sea coast. John Paul Jones did terrorize the British sea coast, but he wasn't a pirate. Jones was the commanding officer aboard a commissioned privateer ship of the United States of America. A privateer ship was given permission by the government to raid enemy merchant ships for profit. Privateering was a very lucrative business. The sailors were allowed to keep half of the prize money captured from enemy vessels. The other half of the money was used in the construction of the fledgling American Navy.

Jones was born in 1747, in Kirkcudbrightshire, Scotland. In 1773, he fled to America on the advice of his friends. He had killed the mutinous ring leader of a ship he was captain of while sailing in the West Indies. The victim had impaled himself on Jones' sword as he ran toward him during a fight. When John Paul was

living in Virginia, he took the last name of Jones to conceal his true identity. After the American Revolution began, Jones was ready to join the rebellion against Britain. He received his naval commission through his friendship with a Continental Congress delegate from North Carolina. The delegate, Joseph Hewes, was a member of the Naval Commission. On December 7, 1775, Jones was commissioned a lieutenant and became the first naval officer to

John Paul Jones
Jones defeated the British warships H.M.S. Drake and the H.M.S. Serapis. He is the father of the American Navy.

★ 31 ★ JOHN PAUL JONES

raise the new Grand Union flag over an American ship. The name of the ship was the Alfred. The Alfred had thirty guns.

In May 1776, Jones received a promotion to captain by Commodore Esek Hopkins. Hopkins was the first Commodore of the United States Navy. Jones took command of the sloop named the Providence. In just one cruise, Jones and his small fleet took sixteen prizes for the Americans.

Jones was soon commanding the warship Ranger. He was ordered by Congress to go to France in 1777. He was to receive a warship that was being built for the United States by Holland. Jones was also carrying the news to France of the grand American victory over General Johnny Burgoyne's British Army at the Battle of Saratoga. Before Jones arrived in France, however, the American delegation in Paris had decided to give the Dutch ship to the French. This act was done as a gesture of friendship. So Jones continued his

command of the Ranger.

On April 10, 1778, Jones sailed from France and started to raid the British coast. His first stop was at a town called Whitehaven. Jones was familiar with this coastal town. He had seen Whitehaven as a boy when he was an apprenticed sailor. Jones and his men rowed ashore. They managed to spike some cannons in the town. Their courage showed the British that they too were vulnerable to attack on their soil. Jones also wanted to kidnap The Earl of Selkirk and ransom his freedom for his fellow Americans being held prisoner. So he decided to attack St. Mary's Isle. St. Mary's Isle is a small peninsula, not far from where Jones grew up. Jones didn't find The Earl, as The Earl was not in town. However, Jones and his men were able to escape back to the sea, leaving the British community dazed at the audacity of the American raiders.

Jones sailed across the Irish Sea. He was still seeking a large

bounty to take back to France as a prize. A strange, surreal event occurred as he calmly sailed into the harbor at Belfast, Ireland. Just a short distance away at anchor was the man-o-war, H.M.S. Drake. The Drake was about to set sail. The captain of the Drake, curious about the unknown ship, sent an investigation party over to the Ranger. Jones was incognito. Jones had yet to unfurl the flag of the United States. He greeted the British boarding party wearing a British officer's uniform. Jones was trying to keep up the appearance of a merchant ship. His ruse worked. The British sailors were promptly made prisoners of war and sent down into the hull of the ship. Then the Ranger started to make her way out to sea. She struck the colors of the United States. The Drake quickly followed. The two warships then sailed far into the open sea. The eighteen gun Ranger was about to be tested in battle for the first time. Her opponent would be the British man-o-war, the H.M.S Drake. The pending battle would be the ultimate test for Captain Jones and the crew of the Ranger. An American warship had never defeated a British warship. The Ranger's eighteen guns were all six-pounders. The Drake had twenty guns, with smaller four-pounders. However, the Drake had many more men onboard. After a day-long chase, the swifter Ranger allowed the Drake to catch up with her. Jones wanted to keep a safe distance from the Drake, so that the numerically superior British forces would not be able to board the Ranger. Jones also wanted to be close enough so that the Ranger's firepower could defeat the enemy. When the battle commenced, the American gunners fired a devastating volley of chain shot and grape shot. This fire power ripped the sails from the masts of the Drake. The American sharpshooters, stationed up in the masts of the Ranger, rained down destruction upon the

British officers on the deck of the Drake. They killed the British first lieutenant, while severely wounding the captain. A British sailor cried out for "Quarter, Quarter!" The British surrendered their ship and the fierce battle was over in little more than an hour. Jones had his prize. The American warship Ranger sailed back to France with the valuable prize of the H.M.S. Drake and a stunning victory over the British Royal Navy.

Nearly one year had passed since Jones had left the French coast to harass the British Isles. It was now February, 1779. Jones was informed that he was to command an older warship called the Duras. The French government had refitted the Duras. Jones renamed her The Bonhomme Richard. This was in honor of Benjamin Franklin's almanac. Franklin's almanac was called "Poor Richard's Almanac." The Bonhomme Richard now had forty guns. The former merchant ship was now a large warship.

In August 1779, Jones and a small squadron of five ships set sail for the British Isles. Jones had a crew of 380 men. His sailors were from several different nations. He had 137 French marines. Portuguese fishermen who supported the American cause were onboard the Bonhomme Richard. There were men from Scotland and Ireland. But most of the crew was from the United States, along with many disgruntled Englishmen who supported the United States.

The Bonhomme Richard was sailing west to east, around the British Isles. Jones and his small flotilla were having success capturing seventeen ships. Jones, however, was not having success with the other captains of his squadron. All of the other captains were French and they were jealous of Jones' command. They acted on their own accord. Two went back to France for questionable repairs. The rest set sail at their pace. This type of insubordination was common in the nebulous

⋆ 31 ⋆ JOHN PAUL JONES

relations between the American and French allies in the eighteenth century. Men sometimes refused to take orders from someone they may have disliked, regardless of the reasoning. But Jones sailed onward.

Jones continued to use deception, as he often flew the British Union Jack. The flying of the enemy flag was a common naval ploy in the eighteenth century. By now, all of Britain was aware of the "pirate" John Paul. He was cruising in her coastal waters. To the British, Jones was just a rebel Scotsman. If captured alive, he would have been hung.

The British were out sailing along their coast. They were looking for the Bonhomme Richard. She was off the coast of eastern England. They found her on September 23, 1779. After being spotted, Jones drew one of the larger British warships close to his flagship. Jones was now using another ruse. The captain of the H.M.S. Serapis demanded that Jones

identify himself. There was no answer. Jones was flying no colors. Suddenly, the American flag was hoisted high above the mast of the Bonhomme Richard. The legendary battle between the Bonhomme Richard and the Serapis was about to begin.

The two warships maneuvered into battle-ready position. Shots were fired. The Bonhomme Richard was hit, but incredibly the shots were not fired from the enemy ship Serapis. The allied warship Alliance had fired on Jones! The captain of the Alliance, the Frenchman Landais, who was believed to be crazy at the time, turned on Jones and the Bonhomme Richard! Landais' strange action certainly supports the theory of his insanity. Meanwhile, Landais' treachery was not over! Jones was now in danger of being sunk. Jones moved his ship alongside the Serapis.

The American flag had been ripped from its mast on the first wayward blast from Landais. British Captain

Pearson of the Serapis yelled out to Jones if he was ready to surrender. Jones answered with his famous words, "I have not yet begun to fight." And fight he did. A four-hour battle ensued. Once again, the insane Landais fired a couple shots! These shots were direct hits on the Bonhomme Richard! Landais inflicted a lot of damage on the Bonhomme Richard. Meanwhile, marines from both ships were firing upon each other. Broadsides were exchanged over and over again. American sailors started to board the Serapis. One of the American marines threw a grenade into the powder magazine of the Serapis. The grenade blast caused extensive damage to the Serapis. Pearson, with mercy for his remaining men, eventually struck his colors and surrendered to Captain John Paul Jones.

The Bonhomme Richard was in such bad shape that Jones had to abandon her. The most critical damage had amazingly come from the allied ship,

JOHN PAUL JONES

the Alliance! Jones and the surviving American crew attempted to keep the Serapis seaworthy. They succeeded. With the help of the British prisoners of war, they were able to sail the Serapis to Holland. The United States had won a great battle on the high seas by defeating a large British warship near her homeland.

Jones, now a famous naval hero, set sail to Philadelphia from France. He had hundreds of tons of needed supplies for General George Washington. It was February, 1781. Many of the supplies that Jones brought to General Washington were used in the last battle of the American Revolution at Yorktown, in October 1781.

Captain John Paul Jones returned to France after the war. He died there in 1792. It would be more than one hundred years until his remains were brought home to the United States in 1905. His body now rests in peace and honor in the chapel of the United States Naval Academy in Annapolis, Maryland.

John Paul Jones is the Father of the United States Navy. The memory of his fight lives today at Annapolis.

GEORGE ROGERS CLARK – CONQUEROR OF THE OLD NORTHWEST

No man conquered more territory for the United States than George Rogers Clark. Born in Virginia in 1752, Clark was a rugged frontiersman. At twenty years old, Clark was a war veteran, having fought in Lord Dunmore's War of 1774. Dunmore was the last royal governor of Virginia. Dunmore wanted to punish the Indians for attacking white settlers in the western territories. Virginia had a claim on these territories. Clark, a militia captain, fought for Virginia's claim to the lands of the Old Northwest.

By the time the American Revolution began in 1775, Clark had familiarized himself with the vast tract of wilderness land of the Old Northwest. For almost two years, he traveled and made observations and plans to conquer this land. This land was adjacent to the Ohio River Valley, in the states of Kentucky, Ohio, Illinois, Indiana, Tennessee and Michigan.

Clark was very concerned about the British attempt to stop the American migration westward.

Clark realized the British garrisons of Vincennes, Detroit, and Kaskaskia had to be conquered. In 1777, Clark proposed to patriot Governor Patrick Henry of Virginia that he lead an expedition to capture the British garrisons. Governor Henry and the Virginia Legislature agreed with Clark. They sent him with public orders to protect Kentucky and secret orders to attack Kaskaskia and take Detroit if possible. These orders were so secret that even the United States Congress did not know of these plans. Promoted to major, Clark and his men marched from Virginia. Only Clark knew of the secret orders. They were headed for the Illinois territory and Kaskaskia.

At Detroit, the British had their most western fort in America. From Detroit the British were able to control the Ohio and Mississippi Rivers. They encouraged their Indian allies to wage war upon the American settlers. British

George Rogers Clark
Clark gained vast territories in the Old Northwest for the United States.

32 ★ GEORGE ROGERS CLARK

Lt. Governor Henry Hamilton of Detroit had been buying scalps from the Indians. The bloodthirsty Hamilton, known as the "Hair Buyer," killed American settlers in the Old Northwest by the score. Clark was determined to put an end to this slaughter and gain the territory for Virginia and the United States.

Clark had a small army of 150 men. They were adventurers like him. Clark led them to an island camp near Louisville. The island camp was called Corn Island. Clark and his men camped at Corn Island for several months. During this time, a few reinforcements led by Simon Kenton arrived from Kentucky. It was at Corn Island that Clark told his small army of his real intentions. They were going to wage war on the British outposts of Kaskaskia, Vincennes, and Detroit, and also capture the settlement of Cahokia.

On June 23, 1778, Clark left Corn Island with 175 men. On the second anniversary of the founding of the United States, July 4, 1778, Clark captured Kaskaskia. He surprised the British commander who was in bed asleep. In less than fifteen minutes, the Americans had secured the town. The Americans met no resistance. Not a single shot was fired! The small American Army continued onward toward Cahokia. When Clark arrived in Cahokia, the subjugated French population was overjoyed with the prospects of joining the Americans. Incredibly, for the French, the Americans were driving out their British masters. The people of Cahokia took an oath of allegiance to the United States. Many Frenchmen joined Clark's little army.

On February 7, 1779, Clark marched toward Vincennes. Scouts had informed Clark that the British had marched from Detroit to Vincennes to counter any American move. The British were already there and waiting for the Americans. The British, led by Hamilton "The Hair Buyer," proceeded to strengthen the old fort and renamed it Fort Sackville, after British Colonial Secretary George Sackville.

Major Clark and his men were slowly advancing toward Vincennes. The early thaw had flooded most of the land. The Americans were wading in waist- and sometimes shoulder-high water for three days. Many of the men were becoming weak and ill. They were suffering badly. However, they persevered.

The Americans had finally gained the high, dry ground near Vincennes. They built fires. They rested. A resident of the town, captured by the Americans, was sent to Hamilton with a letter demanding his surrender. Meanwhile, Clark was careful to disguise the number of troops he had. He marched them over and over again, within sight of the British fort. Clark was careful to march his men with a different flag every time to exaggerate the number of soldiers he had. Clark had

GEORGE ROGERS CLARK

believed that he was outnumbered five to one. However, Clark was determined to capture the fort. Hamilton at first refused the demand of surrender. The Americans then attacked the fort, inflicting light casualties on Hamilton's men. Hamilton, meanwhile, had lost many of his Indian allies to desertion. Then, all of Hamilton's French militiamen refused to fight to the death for the British. Hamilton was left with only seventy nine able men. Hamilton had little choice in the eventual outcome of the battle. On February 25, 1779, Hamilton surrendered Fort Sackville and the town of Vincennes. Clark sent Hamilton to Virginia. Hamilton's French militia went home to Detroit. Clark renamed the fort in honor of Virginia's governor. Fort Patrick Henry was now standing as one of the most western forts in the Old Northwest.

Clark never mounted an attack against Detroit. Although Clark made plans to attack Detroit annually, his small army did all it could to secure the land that it had won. Instead, Clark concentrated on holding onto the Illinois territory.

The courage and daring of George Rogers Clark and his small American Army enabled the United States to make a strong claim to all of the Old Northwest territories. When the Treaty of Paris was signed, the territory that Clark con-quered was still in American hands. The British recognized American sovereignty in the Old Northwest. This land is now the states of Kentucky, Ohio, Indiana, Illinois, Tennessee, and Michigan.

Clark continued his influence over the Old Northwest territories after the war. He was on the board that allocated land to settlers. Clark lived to see his younger brother William gain fame as a national hero. William was second in command in the Lewis and Clark expedition of 1804-1806.

George Rogers Clark, an American Revolutionary War hero, died near Louisville, Kentucky in 1818.

MARY LUDWIG HAYS – MOLLY PITCHER

During the American Revolution many women followed their soldier husbands while supporting them in a consorted effort to defeat British rule in America. These dedicated women became known as "camp followers." Incredibly, sometimes a soldier had his whole family travel along with him! All of the brave women, who followed their soldier husbands during the American Revolution, provided the much needed woman-power and worked many essential jobs that a traveling army needed. These women were the nurses who would tend to the wounded and sick. They would procure many of the foods that the army ate. They would mend clothing. They would build up and break down camps. In effect, they were the unpaid personnel of the American Army in the War of Independence.

One of the most celebrated camp followers and heroines of the American Revolution is Mary Ludwig Hays. She is better known

in history as Molly Pitcher. Mary Ludwig Hays was born Mary Ludwig, near Trenton, New Jersey in 1754. The daughter of a German immigrant, Mary Ludwig Hays was a camp follower and a devoted patriot. She was the wife of Continental soldier John Hays. John Hays was an artillery man.

Mary Ludwig Hays spent the terrible winter of 1777-1778 at Valley Forge with her husband. At Valley Forge, she suffered the same privations that the Continental Army suffered. However, she continued in her efforts to maintain a sense of normalcy with her own

Mary Ludwig Hays

She was a courageous soldier who directed artillery during the Battle of Monmouth.

MARY LUDWIG HAYS

work. Mary Ludwig Hays and other camp followers gave the American soldiers the inspiration to continue the fight against British tyranny.

After the long, cold winter at Valley Forge, the Continental Army fought a large battle on June 28, 1778 at Monmouth, New Jersey. At the Battle of Monmouth, Mary Ludwig Hays gained fame for her courage and heroism. On a very hot day, Mary Ludwig Hays filled pitchers of water from a nearby spring for the American soldiers. During the confusion of battle, men would cry out for water and she would bring them water as fast as she could. During the flurry of the battle, one of the soldiers had mistaken Mary's first name for Molly. The soldiers would yell out for a pitcher. "Molly bring me a pitcher," soldiers would demand. Hence, she became known as Molly Pitcher, the

courageous woman who helped keep the American soldiers hydrated at the Battle of Monmouth.

Mary Ludwig Hays' legend as an American heroine only begins, however, with her pitchers of water. As the battle raged on, her husband John Hays fell wounded while firing his cannon at the British positions. It was at this point in the battle that Mary Ludwig Hays took the place of her fallen husband and started to load and fire the cannon herself. She continued in this effort until the battle was over. The Continental Army had fought hard and well at Monmouth and Mary Ludwig Hays was a significant part of this effort. The Americans had held the strong British Army to a draw on that hot summer day. The Battle of Monmouth was an important moral victory for the Continental Army.

Mary Ludwig Hays would be recognized by the Commander-in-Chief General George Washington after the Battle of Monmouth. General Washington commissioned Mary Ludwig Hays as a sergeant for her courage, inspiration, and heroism. Afterward, she helped nurse her wounded husband back to health at their home in New Jersey.

Both Mary Ludwig Hays and John Hays lived to see the nation free from British rule. Throughout the rest of her life, American Revolutionary War heroine Mary Ludwig Hays was known as Sergeant Molly Pitcher. She deservedly and finally received a military pension from the Pennsylvania state government, where she had settled after the war in 1822, for $40 a year.

EPILOGUE

The stories recounted here, in "George Washington's Unsung Heroes," have been retold many times since the end of the American Revolution. However, nearly 230 years later, many of the heroes in these stories have been forgotten. The events described in this book recall the achievements of the brave patriot men and women who fought for a new nation. The new nation of the United States promised them freedom and liberty. But nothing came easy for these patriots – neither the freedom nor the liberty. Nothing was for certain. Everything material that these patriots owned was in jeopardy. Their houses and property were sometimes sacrificed for freedom's cause. Their lives were put into jeopardy. Some paid the ultimate price with the loss of their life, or suffered a debilitating injury. All of George Washington's heroes shared in this common misery. It was a long eight-year struggle.

The Commander-in-Chief General George Washington persevered along with his countrymen and women. While General Washington may have been physically more comfortable at his headquarters, he suffered his own hardships during those long eight years. When the Commander-in-Chief saw the American Army in dire straights, he suffered along with them. General Washington knew he was asking his small army to do the impossible. After all, they were asked to defeat the world's best military. General Washington, meanwhile, had to be a pillar of strength for the United States to prevail. Because of his steadfast leadership, George Washington's unsung heroes did prevail and won a war with their courageous struggle.

Ultimately, what makes George Washington a great man was that he walked away from absolute power, not just once, but twice in his life. The first time he resigned his commission to return to private life as a citizen of his new nation. To the European leaders, this was a stunning concept. Nobody had ever done that. Had not George Washington just won a war where he commanded and yielded complete power? Yet he relinquished power. The second time George Washington gave up the power vested in him is when he refused to run for president for a third term. George Washington felt comfortable that he left the United States in good hands. These were the people he depended upon and loved. These people were his heroes. They were George Washington's unsung heroes.

SOURCES-SUGGESTED READING

Adler, Mortimer J., Moquin, Wayne. "The Revolutionary Years." Chicago, 1976.

Bailey, Thomas A. "The American Pageant. A History of the Republic." Boston, 1956.

Boatner, Mark Mayo. "The Encyclopedia of the American Revolution." New York, 1966.

Callaham, North. "Henry Knox. General Washington's General." New York, 1958.

Ellis, George. "Siege and Evacuation Memorial." Boston, 1878.

Ferling, John. "A Leap in the Dark." New York, 2003.

Fischer, David Hackett. "Paul Revere's Ride." New York, 1994.

Fleming, Thomas J. "Liberty. The American Revolution." New York, 1997.

Fleming, Thomas J. "Now We Are Enemies." New York, 1960.

Fleming, Thomas J. "The Forgotten Victory. The Battle for New Jersey-1780." New York, 1973.

Forbes, Esther. "Paul Revere and The World He Lived In." Boston, 1942.

Frothingham, Richard. "The History of the Siege of Boston and the Battles of Lexington, Concord and Bunker Hill." Boston, 1849.

Havighurst, Walter. "George Rogers Clark, Soldier In The West." New York, 1952.

Kennedy, Mabel Stockwell. "The Stockwell Genealogy." Labanon, N.H. 1983.

Ketchum, Richard M. "Decisive Day. The Battle For Bunker Hill." New York, 1962.

Ketchum, Richard M. "Saratoga. The Turning Point of America's Revolutionary War." New York, 1997.

Leckie, Robert. "George Washington's War. The Saga of the American Revolution." New York, 1992.

Lossing, Benson J. "Seventeen Seventy-Six, Or the War of Independence. A History of the Anglo-Americans." New York, 1847.

Lossing, Benson J. "The Pictorial Field Book of the Revolution." New York, 1851.

Martin, Joseph Plumb. "Yankee Doodle Boy." New York, 1995.

Meltzer, Milton. "The American Revolutionaries. A History in Their Own Words." New York, 1987.

Mousin, Samuel Eliot. "John Paul Jones. A Sailor's Biography." Boston, 1959.

Parsons, Eugene. "George Washington. A Character Sketch." Chicago, 1898.

Stone, William. "Border Wars of the American Revolution." New York, 1843.

Thomas, Evan. "John Paul Jones, Sailor, Hero, Father of the American Navy." New York, 2003.

Tilghman, Lt. Colonel Tench. "Memoirs of Lt. Colonel Tench Tilghman." New York, 1876.

Watson, Henry C. "Camp-Fires of the Revolution, Or the War of Independence." Philadelphia, 1853.

Weems, M.L. "The Life of George Washington, With Curious Anecdotes, Equally Honorable To Himself, And Exemplary To His Young Countrymen." Philadelphia, 1814.

Winsor, Justin. "The Memorial History of Boston." Boston, 1881.

GLOSSARY

Abolitionist – A person opposed to slavery.

Adjutant – A military officer's executive aide or secretary.

Aide-de-Camp – A military officer's executive aide or secretary.

Alarm – To answer a military call by participation.

Anchor Smith – A smith who makes anchors for ships.

Assumption – Following the Revolutionary War, the Federal government assumed all the war debt from every state, including its own debt, by issuing interest-bearing bonds. This policy was instituted by the first Secretary of the Treasury, Alexander Hamilton.

Batteries – A strategically placed unit of artillery.

Blue Book – First training manual of the United States Army. It was created by General Baron von Steuben.

Board of Selectman – Local political governing body of a town or city.

Brevetted – A temporary commission of a high military rank.

Chain shot – Two cannonballs linked by a short chain.

Coercive Acts – Same as Intolerable Acts; British measures designed to punish the people of Boston. It prohibited the loading or unloading of ships in Boston harbor until tea damages from the Boston Tea Party had been paid.

Colonial Legislature – Local elected body of officials answerable to the Royal Governor.

Colony – People who established a political union or bond with the British Government through a charter and by-laws in the new world of America.

Commander-in-Chief – The top-ranked military man.

Committee of Correspondence Same as the Sons of Liberty; a secret society led by patriots fighting against British rule.

Committee of Safety – Same as the Sons of Liberty; a secret society led by patriots fighting against British rule.

Common Man – A citizen without much money or any power.

Congress – Federal legislative body of the United States. At the time of the revolution it consisted of only representa-

tives. It now has two parts since the inception of the United States Constitution: the House of Representatives and the Senate.

Constitution – The foundational code of principles and laws forming the basis of the United States government.

Continental Army – The American Army.

Continental Congress – The first two Congresses of the United States.

Cryptographical – Secret coded words or letters used in covert operations.

Declaration of Independence The document proclaiming the United States of America's official break with the government of Great Britain.

Dragoon – Fast-moving, horse-back-riding soldiers.

Drill Master – Officer or sergeant responsible for training soldiers.

Dueling – Eighteenth century fight with a pistol.

Federalist Papers – Documents in favor of a strong central government. Supported by and written by Alexander Hamilton, John Jay, and James Madison.

GLOSSARY

Flanking Fire – Shots that are fired coming from the side.

Foraging Party – A group of soldiers gathering supplies for the army.

Founding Fathers – A man who either signed the Declaration of Independence, the United States Constitution, or signed an early treaty on behalf of the United States.

French and Indian War – 1756-1763 – The defeat of France by Britain and American colonists for control of Canada.

Frontiersman – A man who lived on the edge of the wilderness. A trail-blazer.

Grand Union Flag – Hybrid flag of thirteen red-and-white-stripes representing the thirteen colonies and later the thirteen states. The British Union Jack is in the canton of the flag, with the cross of St. George representing England and the cross of St. Andrew representing Scotland. It was America's first national flag.

Grape shot – A canister filled with lead shot.

Guerrilla Operations – Small military units employing "hit and run" tactics and strategy.

Hessians – German mercenary soldiers fighting on behalf of the British. They were from the German principalities of Hesse-Hanau or Hesse-Cassel and various other small principalities.

Highway Men – Self-appointed civilian guards sympathetic to the patriot cause.

Inspector General – Officer in charge of the drilling and inspection of the American Army.

Intolerable Acts – British measures designed to punish the people of Boston. It prohibited the loading or unloading of ships in Boston harbor until tea damages from the Boston Tea Party had been paid.

Jagers – Hessian light mobile infantry.

Knowlton's Rangers – Name of the first military special operations regiment of the United States.

Loyalists – An American loyal to Britain. During the revolution it is estimated that one-third of all Americans were loyal or sympathetic to the British.

Marbleheaders – American sailors from General John Glover's regiment.

Martial Law – Rule by military authority.

Martyr – A person who dies for a cause they deeply believe in.

Mason – A Freemason. A member of the Free and Accepted Order of Masons; a fraternal Christian organization.

Mechanic – An eighteenth century tradesman.

Militia – Part-time soldiers, subject only to colonial or state authority. Today, the militia is equal to the National Guard.

Minuteman – American civilian ready at a minute's notice to bear arms for the protection and safety of the country.

Monroe Doctrine – Warned European nations to keep out of the political and military affairs in the Western Hemisphere.

GLOSSARY

Natural Law – All persons are born with certain intrinsic rights that cannot be taken away by any government. These rights include: liberty, pursuit of happiness, democracy, the right to revolution, and popular sovereignty.

Noble Train of Artillery – The men who successfully brought fifty nine cannons from Fort Ticonderoga to Boston, led by Colonel Henry Knox in 1776.

Parliament – British law-making assembly.

Patriot – An American fighting against British rule.

Privateer – An armed ship allowed by the government to attack the merchant fleet of the enemy to gain profit.

Provincial Congress – Legal legislature body of each colony.

Provincial Militia – Colonial Army or Provincial Army; a national guard.

Quartermaster General – Officer in charge of supplies and provisions for the army.

Rabble-rouser – A demagogue. One who stirs up the masses to revolt.

Redoubt – Small earthen fort.

Regulars – British soldiers during the revolution.

Robert's Rangers – Colonial Americans; a special operations brigade during the French and Indian War.

Sappers and Miners – Frontline soldiers who dug trenches and secured land mines. They also built and repaired roads.

Sexton – A minor official of a church.

Sharpshooter – An expert marksman.

Six Nations – Iroquois Federation; a united governmental assembly of the Iroquois tribes of America.

Sloop – Single-masted sailboat.

Sons of Liberty – Secret society led by American patriots against British rule.

Stamp Act – Measure designed to raise tax money with stamps affixed on all printed material as well as several other popular items.

Suffolk Resolves – These resolves or ideas urged the people of Massachusetts to withhold taxes and to form a separate, independent government. They were written by Dr. Joseph Warren.

Supreme Executive Council – The early state legislature of Pennsylvania.

Teamster – A man who drove a wagon.

Tory – An American loyal to Britain.

Townshend Acts – British measure of implementing a new system of raising revenue by custom commissioners.

Writs of Assistance – British measure that enabled custom officers to search warehouses or homes for contraband.

INDEX

References in *italics* denote illustrations. References in **bold** denote subject of chapter.

INDEX

INDEX

INDEX

INDEX

NOTES

Chapter One: Henry Knox-Artillery Chief:

(1) Ellis, George. "Siege and Evacuation Memorial." Boston. Rockwell and Churchill Printers. 1876. Page 20.

Chapter Seven: Daniel Stockwell Jr.-Massachusetts Minuteman:

(1) Kennedy, Mabel Stockwell. "The Stockwell Genealogy." Lebanon, New Hampshire. New Victoria Printers. 1983. Page 72.

Chapter Thirteen: Moses Stockwell-Little Brother Sees Three Surrenders:

(1) Kennedy, Mabel Stockwell. "The Stockwell Genealogy." Lebanon, New Hampshire. New Victoria Printers. 1983. Page 73.

(2) Ibid. Page 73.

(3) Ibid. Page 73.

Chapter Fifteen: Tench Tilghman-Faithful Assistant:

(1) Tilghman, Lt. Colonel Tench. "Memoirs of Lt. Colonel Tench Tilghman, Secretary and Aide to Washington." Compiled and printed by Oswald Tilghman. Albany, New York. 1876. Page 30.

(2) Ibid. Pages 106-107.

(3) Ibid. Page 38.

(4) Ibid. Page 67.

Chapter Twenty Three: Dr. Joseph Warren-Bunker Hill Martyr:

(1) Lossing, Benson J. "Seventeen Hundred and Seventy-Six, Or the War of Independence." New York. Edward Walker Publishing Company. 1847. Page 170.

To contact Marc Stockwell-Moniz, and to find out more
about having him speak to your group,
contact him at:

Telephone Toll-free (866) 858-1812

or (858) 842-1812

Fax (858) 842-1812

Email amrevpub@cox.net

American Revolution Publishing

12514 Mustang Drive
Poway, CA, 92064, USA

www.gwuh.com

American
Revolution
Publishing

Fax Orders:	(858) 842-1812 (Send this form)
Telephone Orders:	Toll-free (866) 858-1812 or (858) 842-1812 (Have your credit card ready)
email Orders:	amrevpub@cox.net
Postal Orders:	American Revolution Publishing
	12514 Mustang Drive
	Poway, CA, 92064, USA

Please send _____ (qty) copies of "George Washington's Unsung Heroes" book.

SHIPPING INFORMATION

Name: _____

Address: _____

City: _____ State: _____ Zip: _____

Telephone: _____

email address: _____

Quantity: George Washington's Unsung Heroes _____ x $15.95 ....$_____

Shipping (choose method)

☐ U.S. $4.00 each book – $2.00 each additional book..$_____

☐ International $9.00 each book – $5.00 each additional book ....$_____

Tax (add 7.75% for orders shipped to CA addresses) ....$_____

Total Order ....$_____

Payment Method: ☐ Cheque   ☐ Credit Card   ☐ Visa   ☐ MasterCard

Card Number: _____

Name on Card: _____Exp. Date: _____

Authorized signature: _____